MODERN DANCE

The Jooss-Leeder Method

MODERN DANCE

The Jooss-Leeder Method

by

JANE WINEARLS

FOREWORD BY RUDOLF LABAN

PREFACE BY A. V. COTON

With 275 drawings
by Peter Krummins
and 11 diagrams

LONDON

ADAM & CHARLES BLACK

SECOND EDITION

FIRST PUBLISHED 1958
SECOND EDITION 1968
REPRINTED 1973
A. & C. BLACK LTD
© 1958, 1967 A. & C. BLACK LTD.

ISBN: 0 7136 0845 5

PRINTED IN GREAT BRITAIN
BY BILLING & SONS LIMITED, GUILDFORD AND LONDON

FOREWORD

By RUDOLF LABAN

OUR endeavour to build up a contemporary form of stage
dancing has been based on new teaching and training methods
for dancers, as well as on ingenious dance inventions and composition. I have watched the happy and successful collaboration
of Kurt Jooss and Sigurd Leeder—the leading protagonists in this
new field and I am very glad that their methods have found so
devoted a chronicler as Jane Winearls. All who know how
difficult it is to catch the essence of such artistic striving in words
which at the same time will quicken appreciation of its spirit of
essential freedom will welcome this book. Its altruistic aim of
helping to spread as widely as possible growing knowledge and
appreciation of the work of Jooss and Leeder in modern stage
dance is part of my own dreams for the future.

I hope Jane Winearls' book will appeal to a wide public. It
has my best wishes for success.

AUTHOR'S NOTE

I AM grateful to Mr. Rudolf Laban for his permission to use certain Scales of Movement and Dynamic Compositions which have been laid down by him in his book, and which have formed the basis of work of the Jooss-Leeder system.

At Mr. Laban's suggestion I am very glad to include the following :

" Rudolf Laban's basic principles of the dynamic order and design harmony of movement were published in 1926 in his book *Choreographie*. All rights and especially that of translation into any other language are reserved. Copyright is held by the publisher Eugen Diderichs, Jena."

In writing the chapter entitled " A Technique for Performance ", Mr. Gerald Wragg derived invaluable assistance from the published work of Dr. Wilfred Barlow, who is Consultant Physician to the Royal Academy of Dramatic Art, in particular from his paper " Anxiety and Muscle-Tension Pain " published in the *British Journal of Clinical Practice* in May 1959.

J. W.

CONTENTS

PREFACE

by A. V. COTON

THE title " Modern Dance " distinguishes those kinds which have been invented, developed, or adapted from various sources during the past half-century and which are clearly marked by an expressive style quite different from that of other forms such as National, Folk, Musical Comedy or Ballet. No-one can say exactly where or when this began, though Isadora Duncan is usually considered the pioneer of this revolutionary theatre movement.

Unlike most other revolutionaries, Modern Dancers (or the greater proportion of those worth taking seriously) do not waste time denigrating or trying to destroy the system against which they revolted. Ballet has its proper function in the Theatre and the apostles and practitioners of Modern Dance think that this newer kind has a place too. As one style of acting, with its ancillary styles of production and stagecraft, will not serve every imaginable dramatic subject, so Modern Dancers consider that Ballet cannot deal satisfactorily with all possible dance-subjects.

Isadora Duncan's revolt was against the sterility that had come upon the Ballet of her day. She made her own kind of dancing, got talked about and, more important, got her ideas talked about even by such balletic giants as Diaghilev and Fokine. She was so busy being a pioneer, making converts, opening new paths that she did not have the time—nor, think many people, the talent—to create a teaching method for her dance-style, which died either with, or very soon after, her. The whole cultural and artistic atmosphere of Europe and America was at this time ripe for a continuance of her pioneering work and many original thinkers, researchers and idealists laboured, in their various ways, to follow further along the path she had indicated. The record of their work is as fine as that done in any other field of artistic research. The best of them studied and re-studied, as few traditional *maitres-de-ballet* ever did, every sort of knowledge which might start a new line of thought ; the history of dancing, of philosophy, of mathematics, and the sciences of acting, gesture, athletics, acrobatics, were made to yield up notions on the functions of timing, rhythm, space, harmony, which were then experimented with until some point was proved or disproved.

All this has occurred within a space of about sixty years and, in this period, the lives and careers of Rudolf Laban, Mary Wigman, Kurt Jooss, Sigurd Leeder in Europe, and of Ruth St. Denis, Ted Shawn, Martha Graham, José Limon, Doris Humphrey in America, are records of ceaseless probing, enquiry, experiment, all equally remarkable for the degree of honesty and selflessness inspiring them. In fact the best training methods of Modern Dance are systems as coherent and logical as the system of ballet training ; many of the Moderns accept parts of the technique of ballet, or learn, and then use, its technique in new adaptations fitted for their dancing.

Once we can begin to look at the best work in this field without comparing every aspect of it with ballet, it is clear that Modern Dance has brought a new kind of vitality into the larger art of Theatre Dancing ; it is as logical a growth as the parallel series of experiments that have occurred in such arts as music, painting, sculpture and poetry within the same period.

Part of the legacy of Duncan—for, like all great innovators, her work and reputation have suffered from the excesses committed by the more thoughtless and selfish of her disciples or converts—is a vast regiment of people who can claim (there exists no patenting process to protect the genuine) the name of Modern Dancer, but who are quite unworthy of serious consideration. Usually they are the kind who, in innocent and unsophisticated ways, try to do as Duncan did—to dance freely, spontaneously, out of exuberance and idealism. As she appeared to dispense with any elaborate technical method, so they too imagine that " the urge to self expression " is, in itself, good enough as an apparatus. The record of this kind of Modern

Dancer is a burden to be lived down by those who approach their work fully understanding the need to train hard in methods as hard as those belonging to the province of ballet dancing.

Modern Dance, to have any meaning for the spectator or value for the dancer, must be taught as exactly and as continuously as the older method. We assume the existence of natural laws concerning weight, speed, balance, harmony, in the human body and if the dancer is to use that body expressively in a theatre he must be trained to a knowledge of how, when, and how much he will use those laws.

The greater part of Modern Dance development in Europe (in America it started from a different appraisal of the laws of physical movement) grows logically and quite consistently from Rudolf Laban's work as a movement-experimenter. Beginning with studies of ballet, of the work of Delsarte, of many kinds of folk dance, of the laws of mathematics and geometry, he evolved a means of " dissecting out " the basic elements which *create and control* every kind of movement of which the human anatomy is capable. No-one, least Laban himself, pretends that everything knowable has been revealed ; some of his fellow researchers have, at various points, agreed to disagree with his findings, and have pursued other routes. His work was furthered by the collaboration of Kurt Jooss and Sigurd Leeder, who starting with the methods and experiments promoted by Laban, carried movement research further until there was evolved the Jooss-Leeder method whereby the dancers of the Ballets Jooss were trained. The importance of this company for over a quarter of a century in the field of Modern Dance is an indication of the value of this method.

There can be no short cut to success in any kind of Theatre Dancing and the aspiring Modern Dancer needs the same stern discipline, regular work, and devoted commitment to his task as the student of ballet must show. Modern Dance methods, like those of Ballet, can be used to train people who have, perhaps, neither ambition nor talent enough to make a professional career. There is too much propaganda which insists that a period of ballet training, whether elementary or intensely advanced technically, is the " best method " of teaching young people how to use their bodies sensibly, dynamically, rewardingly. Modern Dance methods, though unbacked by the glamour (and the disillusion, too) that goes with training in a system of ballet, can give a control, a flexibility, a lyricism, as understandable and usable as those conferred by the same amount of training in ballet.

The method discussed in this book is that of the Jooss-Leeder system, particularly as now taught in the Sigurd Leeder School. The elements of movement, the basic laws of body expressiveness, and the methods of co-ordinating them are here analysed and explained in easily comprehensible terms. The book's purpose is to provide teacher or student of Modern Dance with a practical training method in the Jooss-Leeder style. One of its greatest values will be the clarifying of this particular method for those who have watched, or attempted to study, one of the systems of Modern Dance which has, so far, not been coherently and comprehensively set down on paper. There may be a risk of some misunderstandings arising from the setting down of a method whose basic principles are still not fully realised ; but there is something to be gained by setting down in this clarified form what is known structurally of a dance-method which has been taught logically for nearly thirty years, and which has shown itself completely valid as an expressive style in the contemporary Theatre.

INTRODUCTION

IF you were to ask the question to-day in England, " What is Modern Dance ? ", the answers would be very widely varied. This is due to several factors.

The influence of Duncan showed itself here at the beginning of the century, in the work of Ruby Ginner, Madge Atkinson and Margaret Morris, and although these three pioneer teachers were interested in the Theatre, and were themselves trained dancers, their work was very much more active in Educational, Recreational and Remedial fields. They shared a belief in the value and necessity of freeing the body from unnatural and even harmful demands of a highly specialised technique, and gave an important place in their systems, to the study of natural rhythms as a basis of improvisation. Unlike the Free Dancers of Europe and America, these three teachers kept closely to the Greek ideal that originally inspired Duncan, and incorporated in their methods, many set body designs taken from Greek Vases and Sculpture.

The many styles of Free Dance arising outside England came from the basic concept of regarding the individual dancers' body as the means through which a technique must be found. The pitfalls of this conception are obvious. At top level, spontaneity and creative experiment, undeviating search for the right artistic means, and constant research and practice in other art forms, result in a richness that is impossible within the confines of one narrowly specialised technique. At any other level, a great deal of formless self-expression and technical incompetence, can be passed off as Modern in dancing as in any other art form.

Creative experiment within a method presents the difficulty of avoiding an unconscious selection of familiar patterns which become an improvisation of means rather than a spontaneous response. The idea of creating a movement for oneself out of a purely spontaneous reaction is difficult to accept, when a number of expressive patterns have already been set down.

The work of Ann Driver (like that of Dalcroze), is based upon fundamental elements, but movement that is always bound by a musical pattern leaves little more room for creative activity than that bound by the pattern of a dance method.

The greatest impact that Laban's work made in England was in Education. He came here at a time when activity methods were replacing formal instruction wherever possible, and Physical Education had to make the same adjustment. Through the untiring work of Laban's colleague, Lisa Ullmann, the Education Authorities accepted his Basic Classification of Movement Analysis as the foundation for the teaching of special technical skills, and Modern Dance as an integral part of the creative development of child and student in relation to the community. It is now a required subject in Teacher Training Colleges, and the Art of Movement Studio, of which Lisa Ullmann is Founder and Principal, deals mainly with Educational Modern Dance.

The situation in the Theatre is very different. England is the stronghold of Classical Ballet, and although the Free Dance has had some influence on choreography, the core of the training and the conventions of attitude remain unchanged. Modern Dance has had to rely upon the sort of work featured by Films, Musicals and Television, importations from America, and visiting Ballet Companies. One or two valiant individuals have tried to support semi-professional groups or earn a reputation as recital dancers. This arduous task is made almost impossible by the unbridged gap between Educational and Theatrical Dance in England.

In America, Europe and Japan, Professional Modern Dance Groups are given status and support, and the professional dancer is accepted and recognised as a teacher in schools and colleges. There are Dance Faculties in the Universities, and school teachers continue their own dance education by performing with professionals. In this way both the professional and the educationalist are enriched.

Attempts have been made here to adapt Classical Ballet for Education, but these have been unsuccessful in gaining the support of the authorities. Occasional visits to the Ballet are arranged for school children, so that the best of our Dance Culture can be enjoyed by the few who are able to understand and appreciate it. There is, however, a wilderness between what is experienced by the child and student in Educational Modern Dance in school and college, and what can be seen at top artistic level in the Theatre.

Professional Modern Dance of the quality of Ballet Jooss, Martha Graham, José Limon, and one or two small groups built round reputable soloists, can be seen possibly twice in a generation.

This is the situation that makes it impossible in England to give a clear answer to the question, " What is Modern Dance ? " Between Educational Modern Dance and the American Modern Dance of the entertainment world, there is room for an artistic whole which can link the class room with the stage, and educate the person whilst training the dancer. This I believe the work of Sigurd Leeder to do. Since he established his London School in 1947, five hundred students, including dancers, actors, film stars, school teachers and business girls, have passed through his hands. The Jooss-Leeder Method has been taught all over the world, and has helped to bridge the gap between dance as an Educational activity, and dance as a fully matured art of the Theatre.

In offering this book as a guide to the professional dancer and teacher, I am well aware of the dangers. I hope, however, that it may serve to assist those who have met the many variations of Free or Modern Dance outlined above, to a clearer under-standing of the individual freedom possible within a Dance Technique which has been founded upon scientific research and human observation and understanding.

It is set down also to preserve, in its technical form, the joint work of Kurt Jooss and Sigurd Leeder, who have developed this method from the inspiration and fundamentals of Rudolf Laban.

3. Sinking to the floor after continued activity.

4. The rising from the keyboard of a pianist's hands after excessive tension.

(3)

Assistance of Gravity producing Heaviness.

(4)

Assistance of Gravity producing Softness.

Under normal circumstances the cycle of Tension and Relaxation follows the same pattern as that of breathing. This can be likened to the blowing up of a balloon followed by a slow deflation.

The outward expansion of the diving movement shown in Illustration 1 and the sinking movement in Illustration 3, could follow one another continuously as an example of the basic cycle of normal Tension and Relaxation.

Under abnormal conditions, such as those causing great physical or emotional strain, the breathing cycle of expansion and deflation becomes more like a sponge being squeezed strongly and then being released so that it can resume its normal state. The Tension and Relaxation cycle that follows this pattern can be seen in Illustrations 2 and 4. In both cases a strong contraction is followed or preceded by a release.

From these two breathing patterns, the basic laws of Tension and Relaxation can be studied.

1. Tension as outward expansion results in lightness.

2. Tension as inward contraction results in strength.

3. Relaxation as inward deflation results in heaviness.

4. Relaxation as outward release results in softness.

This can be tabulated for clarity.

Diagram 1

	TENSION			RELAXATION	
1	LIGHT	EXPANSION	**3**	HEAVY	DEFLATION
2	STRONG	CONTRACTION	**4**	SOFT	RELEASE

It will be seen from a practical study of Tension and Relaxation that movement continually flows in its process of change, from lightness to heaviness, or from strength to buoyancy. In doing so, gravity is either assisting the flow of movement or is being resisted by it. In order to achieve economy in movement, it is necessary to experience the difference between weight as an assisting factor and strength as a resistance. For purposes of classification, this can be established as the second principle.

PRINCIPLE TWO. WEIGHT AND STRENGTH [1]

When the force of gravity is being overcome by energy, it can be said that Weight is being resisted. If a great deal of energy resistance is used, the resulting movement will be strong. If the minimum amount of energy resistance is offered, the resulting movement will be light. In either case the movements will contain tension as they are offering resistance to weight in some degree.

In making use of Weight, energy can be greatly assisted, and economic movement will balance strength with weight. In giving way to gravity it can be said that Strength is being given assistance. If a great deal of gravity assistance is given the resulting movement will be heavy. If only a little gravity assistance is given, the resulting movement will be soft. In either case the movements will contain relaxation as they are being assisted by gravity in some degree. This can be tabulated in the same way as Principle One.

Diagram 2

STRENGTH				WEIGHT	
1	LIGHTNESS	A LITTLE RESISTANCE	**3**	HEAVINESS	A GREAT DEAL OF ASSISTANCE
2	STRENGTH	A GREAT DEAL OF RESISTANCE	**4**	SOFTNESS	A LITTLE ASSISTANCE

Principle I, Tension and Relaxation, and Principle II, Weight and Strength, will be seen to have great bearing upon one another. Tension is constantly flowing into relaxation and relaxation into tension. Strength is constantly changing into weight and weight into strength. Upon this foundation the whole structure of movement study and dance arises.

[1] See Author's Note, page 6.

PRINCIPLE THREE. THE THREE BASIC RHYTHMS [1]

A single movement can be defined as a change from one state to another in response to a stimulus. In making this change, the aim of the movement can be either to leave the present state or to reach the new one. The accent of effort will be placed on that part of the movement which contains the aim. It may also be possible that the stimulus to change from one state to another is given only for the sake of making the change. In this case the aim is neither to leave the present state, nor to reach the new one, but to keep in a state of motion between the two. In this case the accent of effort would fall on that part of the movement between its beginning and its end. Musically, these three accents can be written thus—

For purposes of classification we can divide all movements into three rhythmic groups according to where the accent occurs.

1. Initial.   2. Terminal   3. Transitional

Initial Accent. Movements which have their accent at the beginning seek only to leave the present state. Tension is gathered suddenly and immediately released with an explosive action, the rest of the movement being the resulting follow through of the initial action. Whatever the degree of tension, whether it be light or strong, movements with an initial accent are of an impulsive nature.

Examples :

(5) *Tossing the head.*   (6) *Snatching oneself away from someone's grasp.*

[1] See Author's Note, page 6.

Terminal Accent. Movements in this group have their accent at the end and seek to achieve a definite purpose in attaining a new state. Tension is gathered throughout the movement and comes to a final climax as the purpose is achieved. The rest of the movement is the flow back in order to repeat the action. Whatever the degree of tension, whether it be light or strong, movements with a terminal accent are of a purposeful nature.

Examples :

(7) *Turning the head sharply to focus upon an object.*

(8) *Thrusting out the foot to intercept an object.*

Transitional Accent. Between the Initial Accent and the Terminal Accent there is a transitional accent which connects the beginning and the end of a movement. This forms a pendulum like swing which keeps in constant motion between two points. In themselves, pendulum movements are not progressive but can be used to create momentum for movements in the other two categories. Strength and Weight are balanced in such a way that the accent falls upon the transition between the two, i.e., where weight becomes strength, in the middle part of the movement. Whatever the quality of swing, whether strong or light, movements with a transitional accent are of harmonious and regular nature.

Example :

(9) *Use of pendulum swing in arms and legs in walking.*

Diagram 3

THREE BASIC RHYTHMS

INITIAL
ACCENT

TRANSITIONAL

ACCENTS

TERMINAL
ACCENT

As will be seen when studying the diagram, these three basic classifications of rhythm are a means whereby to clarify the balanced relationship between tension and relaxation, strength and weight, in order to arrive at a clearer understanding of the rhythmic use of the body. As stated in the introduction to Principal I, the underlying rhythmic cycle of all life forms is a waxing and waning of energy. Both are living forces and one is constantly flowing into the other. A simple analogy is that of the accelerator in a motor-car. When pressing on the accelerator with the foot, more power is gained for speed on a flat surface or strength uphill. When easing gradually the pressure of the foot, the power is diminished and less speed is attained on the flat or less strength used downhill. The point to be made is that even while power is decreasing, the car is in action all the time. Relaxation in movement should be regarded as a living force out of which a climax of tension may be achieved steadily and harmoniously. It must therefore be a consciously controlled diminishing of power rather than an uncontrolled collapse separating movements of aggressive tension. Tension in movement should be regarded as an increase of power culminating in the climax of activity, which is reached immediately before the expending or diminishing begins.

Comparing with Diagram 3, the whole cycle may be represented by a series of waves.

Diagram 4

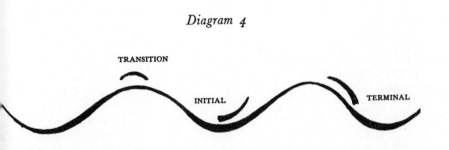

Here can be seen the continuous flow of movement between the momentary suspension of activity at the peak of the wave and the momentary cessation of activity at the trough. In both moments, Tension and Relaxation are balanced. At the peak of activity a moment of complete poise is achieved, when the body is at its most vital and perfect equilibrium attained. This can be seen in the action of a dive.

(10) *Here Tension and Relaxation are perfect partners.*

During the moment of cessation of activity, at the trough of the wave, a recreative pause is reached when the body is at its most receptive and therefore most potentially powerful.

Tension and Relaxation can be regarded as the results of the effect of Gravity upon the body, but there are also external forces and conditions which affect the quality of action within the body, and change the rhythmic pattern.

Examples :

(11) *Walking on ice where the natural flow of movement is impeded and careful guidance is necessary.*

(12) *Walking on springy turf where the natural resilience of the body is aided.*

This adjustment of the natural flow of movement in the body to meet varying conditions is dealt with in Principle Four.

PRINCIPLE FOUR. FLOW AND GUIDANCE

Some actions are free flowing by nature, as in flicking round with a duster. Some are more naturally guided, like ironing. Many actions can be free flowing or guided.

Examples :

(13) *Throwing things about in order to unearth a mislaid object —Free flowing.*

(14) *Throwing at a target— Guided.*

In bodily movement therefore, Guidance is the result of a certain conscious deliberation and in dance movement must take its place with Free Flow. As with Tension and Relaxation, Strength and Weight, there must be a rhythmic swing between freedom and control.

These broad Principles of Movement are intended as a basis upon which to build a progressive method of professional dance training and a means by which highly stylised skills can be analysed in terms of their essentials.

All living things have danced from the beginning of time. In the widest sense every human being has danced somewhere or at some time, even if only in the eyes or in the heart. Spontaneous outpouring of feeling through movement is Dance in this sense, but in order to be, not only a means of self-expression, but also a clearly articulated means of communication, Dance must accept the restraint and discipline of the laws of balance and design common to all Art forms.

Movement has its own laws of dynamics and design upon which Dance Technique is based. In the method of training out-lined in this volume, the classification of these laws fall into three sections.

1. Technique. 2. Dynamics. 3. Direction-and-Design.

CHAPTER II

TECHNIQUE

FOOT POSITIONS

THESE are the five positions standardised by the Classical Ballet together with the open and closed diagonals. The weight is equally divided between the feet and in open positions a distance of approximately one foot length is left between the feet. All the positions are determined by the relationship of the legs to the centre line of gravity.

(15)
First Position.

(16)
Second Position.

(17)
Third Position.

(18)
Fourth Position.

(19)
Fifth Position.

(20)
Open Diagonal.

(21)
Crossed Diagonal.

RELATIONSHIP OF THE LEGS

In First and Second positions the legs are on a line passing from side to side through the centre.

In the Third position, the legs are on a diagonal line passing through the centre.

In the Fourth and Fifth positions the legs are in a forward and back line passing through the centre of the body.

The Open and Closed Diagonals are an extension of the Third position.

The Classical Ballet has established the turn out of the leg from the hip socket. Other forms of dance have advocated a forward facing or even an inturned foot. For expressive purposes, infinite variations and adaptations will be necessary, but the five positions and the diagonals are the foundations upon which the dancer's technique is built, wherever the foot faces.

SUPPORT AND GESTURE

These are terms mainly referring to the legs and feet, but it is possible in dancing to support the body upon any part of the anatomy. When standing naturally, with the weight upon both feet (as in any of the basic positions illustrated above) one is said to be in double support. While standing upon one leg only, one is said to be in single support. It is also possible, of course, to have more weight upon one leg than the other. This would be referred to as half support on the leg taking less weight.

The term Gesture is used for the movement of the leg that is not in the act of taking any weight. It may be touching the floor, but must not be receiving any of the weight at the time the gesture is being made.

Examples :

(22) *Single Support left leg, Gesture right leg.*

(23) *Single Support right leg, Gesture with toe touch, left leg.*

Both legs in Gesture. This is either a
jump or a supporting of weight on another
part of the anatomy, as in hanging from a
beam.

(24) *Double Gesture.*

Example :

LEVELS

The weight can be supported at three main levels.

High : Standing on the toes.

Unless a very high or very low lifting of the heels is required,
this support level is taken to be upon the ball of the foot with
the heel actively lifted. Any other degree must be especially
indicated.

Medium : Standing upon the full foot.

Deep : Standing upon the full foot with knees bent.

(25)
Double High Support.   (26)
Double Medium Support.   (27)
Double Deep Support

When transferring Weight from one leg to another, it can be done through any of the Support Levels.

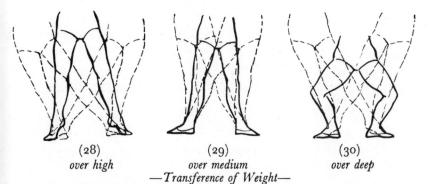

(28)
over high

(29)
over medium

(30)
over deep

—Transference of Weight—

There are three main gesture levels, which can be taken in any direction.

High Gesture : Leg raised to point as high as possible above horizontal. Forwards or sideways. (It is not anatomically possible to achieve High Gesture backwards or sideways without tilting the pelvis.)

(31) *Forwards High Gesture.*

Medium Gesture : Leg raised to point horizontally. Forwards, sideways or backwards (the latter with pelvis tilt).

(32) *Forwards Medium Gesture.*

Deep Gesture : Leg raised to point downwards towards the ground.   Forwards, sideways or backwards.

(33) *Forwards Deep
        Gesture.*

It is possible to refer to support and gesture on the same leg. This occurs in two cases.

(*a*) Landing from a jump with legs in a maintained gesture. The gesture is made during the flight and kept as the landing is made.

(*b*) Making a gesture with the leg upon which the weight has already been taken.

In both cases, the resulting final position is the same.

(34) *High Support with Deep Gesture.*

Many variations and combinations of Support, Gesture, Levels, and Transference of weight can be found in co-ordination with the foot positions.

ARMS, HANDS AND HEAD

Although it is possible to stand upon the hands, arms or head, for purposes of Dance Classification, these members are considered to be in Gesture and are described in the same terms as the Leg Gestures, i.e., by Level and Direction.

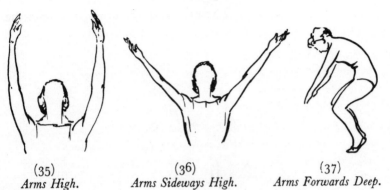

(35)
Arms High.

(36)
Arms Sideways High.

(37)
Arms Forwards Deep.

Hands are classified by the direction in which the palms are facing.

(38)
Palm Deep.

(39)
Palm Forwards.

(40)
Palm High.

The Head is also classified by Level and Direction when the whole head tilts.

(41)
Head Backwards High.

(42)
Head Sideways High.

When a rotation occurs, however, the movement is described by the direction towards which the face is turned.

(43)
Head Sideways Left.

Further classification of Arms, Hands, Legs and Feet are included in the next section.

BASIC STEPS AND JUMPS

A step is a combination of a Support, a Gesture and a Transference of Weight, when the body is supported either on one leg or the other, or between the two. For example—Stand with double support in a first position. Move the right leg forward in gesture to the fourth position. Transfer the weight slowly on to the right foot, leaving the left leg in gesture in a rear fourth position. Transfer the weight slowly on to the right foot, leaving the left leg in gesture in a rear fourth position. During this transference of weight, there will be a moment of double support. Move the left leg in gesture from the rear fourth position to the forward fourth position and transfer the weight on to it, leaving the right leg in gesture in a rear fourth position. Close the right leg by gesture to the left, and stand with Double Support. Perform all this at medium Level.

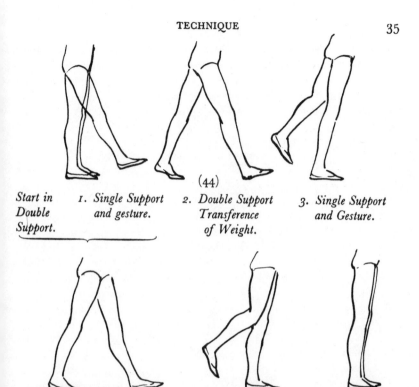

| Start in Double Support. | 1. Single Support and gesture. | 2. Double Support Transference of Weight. | 3. Single Support and Gesture. |

(44)

4. *Double Support Transference of Weight.*   5. *Single Support and Gesture.*   6. *Double Support Close.*

In this sequence only one Full Step has been taken. From Double Support at the beginning (1) to Single Support and Gesture (3) is only a Half Step as the weight has been carried from the centre line of the body to one side, i.e., from two feet to one. Here the Full Step begins at (3) and finishes at (5), when a full transference of weight has been made from one foot on to the other, i.e., from one side, through the centre to the other side. The sequence finishes with another Half Step, when the weight is carried from one foot on to two. This analysis of walking or stepping into Full Step and Half Step, taken in combination with variations of Support, Gesture, Support Levels and Changes of Direction, forms the basis of all Dance Steps that do not leave the ground.

Running is essentially different from walking in that it does not have the moment of double support during the transference of weight from one foot to the other. Instead it has a moment in mid air when both legs are in gesture, i.e., not supporting the body, as the weight is thrown off the back foot on to the front foot in a leap.

(45) *Double Gesture (leap).*

Variations upon leaping, hopping and jumping form the basis of all dance steps when combined with Full and Half Steps. Basically only five fundamental jumps are possible.

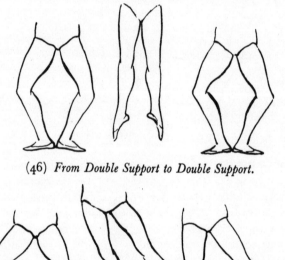

(46) *From Double Support to Double Support.*

(47) *From Double Support to Single Support.*

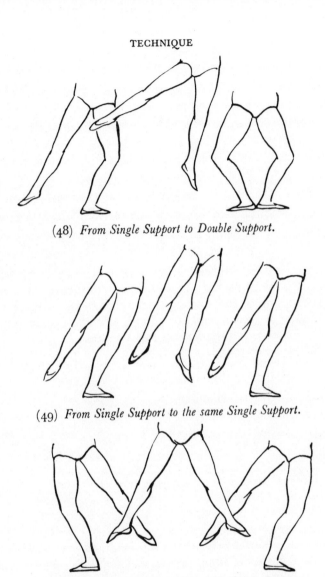

(48) *From Single Support to Double Support.*

(49) *From Single Support to the same Single Support.*

(50) *From Single Support to the other Single Support.*

Combinations of all the foregoing steps and jumps taken in co-ordination with variations of Support, Gesture, Support Levels and Change of Direction form the basis of all dance steps and sequences.

STARTING POINTS AND GUIDANCE

The foregoing sections have been mainly concerned with the placing of weight upon the supports, and the position of arms and head in relation to the body, but now a further classification becomes necessary.

Anatomically the body is capable only of certain movements. These are determined by :

1. The structure of the joint upon which the muscles operate.
2. The order or sequence in which the joints go into activity.

These are the foundations of all anatomical possibilities of the body.

Starting Points are defined as being the place where the *external* movement is seen to start. It is of course understood that many *unseen* muscles must come into operation before the limb, trunk or head is able to move, but a detailed study of anatomy and physiology is outside the scope of this volume. It is sufficient to establish the following.

Arms.—There are three possible starting points.

1. Shoulder
2. Elbow
3. Hand.

Example 1.

Lifting the arms sideways medium with a starting point in the shoulder. This gives a developing wave-like movement of the arms. If in lowering the arms, the shoulder is again the starting point, the same wave-like motion will be seen, and raising and lowering can follow each other in uninterrupted snake-like ripples. Raising and lowering both start in the shoulder which is a ball and socket joint. It is this that gives the particular rounded undulation to the whole movement. The next joint to go into action is the elbow, which being a hinge joint, brings the upper and lower arm together or apart. Finally the combination of small joints which form the wrist become active, and complete the raising of the arm sideways by bringing the hand into line.

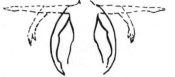

(51) *Arm lift starting in shoulder.*

Example 2.

Lifting the arm sideways medium with starting point at the hand. This gives a placed precision to the movement as though reaching for an object. The fingers are lifted, drawing the lower arm forwards, upwards and sideways. The elbow then follows causing the upper arm to lift, until the whole arm is sideways medium from the shoulder. The return movement is done in the same way. The hand brings the lower arm forwards, towards and downwards to the side of the body from where the fingers are lifted again to repeat the movement.

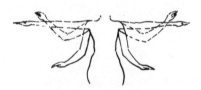

(52) *Arm lift starting at the hand.*

Example 3.

Lifting the arm sideways medium with starting point at the elbow. This gives a stilted angularity to the movement. Since the elbow is the connecting point between the upper and lower limb it must affect both parts of the arm. In starting a sideways lift of the arm, the elbow draws the upper arm sideways and upwards from the shoulder, while the lower arm hangs passively downwards. When the movement reaches its limit, the lower arm is then lifted sideways.

(53) *Arm lifting sideways in two parts.*

It will be seen by comparing these three examples that although the final position was the same, the means by which it was reached was different. The character of each movement has been given by the starting point of the movement and the order in which the joints have followed the action. In the first two examples there was a simple sequence of flow from shoulder to elbow to hand, or from hand to elbow to shoulder. This can conveniently be called a *Sequential Movement*.

The third example has two separate halves to its movement and could easily be stopped in the middle as there is no follow through necessary to complete the movement. The final position was in fact the result of two isolated consecutive movements. This can conveniently be called *Isolated Movement*. It becomes a matter of choice whether more than one isolated movement is made.

In all examples there was a clearly visible starting point and a final position reached. There is, however, a fourth way in which the arms can be lifted sideways.

Example 4.

Lifting the arms sideways medium in one straight line. Here the wrist joint is fixed in order to carry the lower arm sideways, and the elbow joint is fixed in order to carry the upper arm sideways. There cannot be said to be a starting point so much as a guiding area since the arm is moved in one piece (by the co-ordination of all three joints). This movement can conveniently be called *Co-ordinated Movement*.

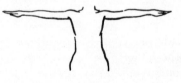

(54) *Arm lifting sideways as a whole.*

Comparison of these four examples will reveal the following :

Sequential Movement is one in which the activity at the starting point is followed immediately by activity in each of the next joints along the natural line of the limb, to secure a continuous flow of movement.

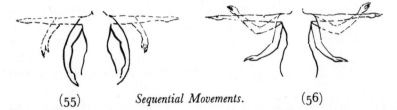

(55)   *Sequential Movements.*   (56)

Isolated Movement is one in which the movement at the starting point terminates when the range of the joint is reached, and no other joint action follows. Another isolated movement can be added at will, but is not an essential part of the original movement. There would then be two Consecutive Isolated Movements.

(57) *Isolated Movements.*

Co-ordinated Movement is one in which all joints work together at the same time in order to move the limb as a whole.

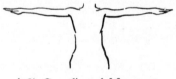

(58) *Co-ordinated Movement.*

In all the foregoing examples another factor must be considered ; that of *Guidance*. When joints go into action, they move the limb or part of a limb into one direction or another so that one of its surfaces is facing the direction of the movement.

For example, if the left arm is held straight out in front of the body with the thumb uppermost and the little finger facing downwards, it can be moved to the right side across the body, or to the left away from the body.

When moving the arm to the right across the body, the inner surface of the arm is leading the movement. When the arm is moved to the left away from the body, the outer surface of the arm is leading the movement. This function of leading is referred to as *Guidance*.

Examples :

 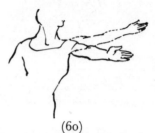

(59)	(6o)
Inside Guidance of the Arm.	*Outside Guidance of the Arm.*

Other surfaces of body and limbs can lead a movement.

Examples:

(61)	(62)	(63)
Palm Guidance.	*Cut Guidance.*	*Chest Guidance.*

(with the thumb edge of the hand)

Starting Points and Guidance are inter-dependent and it will sometimes be more convenient to use one term than the other. In either case, the joint or surface area is leading the movement.

TRUNK AND HEAD

The Spine is a combination of joints round which the Trunk moves, and it is capable of every movement made by the joints of the limbs. Broadly the Trunk is divided into three sections.

> Upper Section—Shoulder Girdle
> Middle Section—Waist
> Lower Section—Pelvic Girdle.

Each of these areas can lead the movement of the Trunk.

Examples :

Turning into a step.—
(64) *With Hip leading.*

(65) *With Shoulder leading.*

(66) *With Waist leading.*

(67) *All in one piece.*

Many patterns of movement can be found in the body by varying and combining Starting Points, Leading Part and Guidances, and each will bring its own character to the movement. In a later section more details will be given about joint action and its characteristics.

SCOOPING AND STREWING

This is a convenient name given to a sequence of movements made by the arms and legs which form a continuous pattern in relation to the Trunk. They are based upon a swinging fall of the limbs towards and away from the centre line of the body. In falling, the limb gathers weight which is then either caught up and held on the rise, or caught up and scattered on the rise. Scooping is the name given to the movement which gathers strength from the fall and holds it. This is usually done in its simplest form towards the centre line of the body. It is possible to scoop away from the body, but this necessitates a rotation in the whole limb. Scooping can also be done at any level.

Stand with the arms lifted sideways, elbows dropped a little, fingers lifted, palms facing out. Allow the elbows to fall heavily inwards and downwards while the shoulder joint rotates outwards. Continue immediately on the same impetus by swinging the hand and forearm inwards and upwards across the chest. This will lift the elbow and upper arm forward a little. Maintain the position reached by holding the strength gathered on the swing.

Strewing is the name given to the swinging fall which gathers weight in order to scatter it on the rise. In its simplest form this is done away from the centre line of the body, although, by means of a rotation of the whole limb, it is possible to strew towards the centre. Strewing, like Scooping, can be done at any level.

Example :

Start with the arms across the chest as at the end of Scooping. Allow the elbows to fall heavily backwards and downwards while the shoulder joint rotates outwards. Continue immediately on the same impetus, to fling the hand and forearm downwards and up to the side. This will carry the whole arm outwards and upwards. Immediately the impetus of the gathered weight is expended, the elbow will fall, bringing the whole arm down by the side of the body.

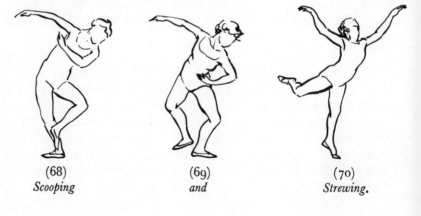

(68)	(69)	(70)
Scooping	*and*	*Strewing.*

It will be seen that the two movements are complementary. By repeating alternate Scooping movements towards the centre and Strewing movements away, the Trunk and Head can participate in a vast rhythmic inswing and outswing, which gives a sense of great exhilaration and freedom.

When taken with the legs, scooping and strewing follows the same joint action, but the same freedom of limb is obviously not possible. While the weight is supported on one leg, the free leg can perform scooping and strewing gestures continuously.

Example :

Stand on the right leg with left lifted sideways. Drop the pelvis downwards and backwards on the left side letting the upper leg fall downwards and forwards across the centre line of the body, pointing the toes downwards as the foot leaves the floor. This will cause the knee to rise forwards. This is the scoop. Allow the knee to fall and the hip and pelvis to return to normal until the toes and ball of the foot slide into the floor just beside and in advance of the supporting leg. Rotate the hip inwards, lifting the pelvis forward and upward on the left side, and push the foot sideways, backwards and upwards away from the centre line of the body. This is the strew. Allow the foot to fall into a toe touch gesture into second position and repeat the scoop. Throughout the movement of the gesture leg, the supporting leg must be kept fluid and follow the fall and rise of the movement, by pliancy in the knee joint.

(71)
Scooping *and* *Strewing* (72)
with the Leg.

It is possible to combine arms and legs in many ways and to make endless variations in co-ordination with steps, jumps, levels and change of direction.

In the study and practice of Scooping and Strewing, it will be found that the two movements, being complementary, act as a rhythmic preparation for one another. When taken in this way, where Scooping is used as a preparation for Strewing, a tremendously vigorous outswing can be achieved on the Strewing action if combined with a jump.

Variations of steps and jumps can be used as a basis for the preparatory Scooping of the outswing and the Strew can be combined with turning. All variations of Scooping and Strewing should be used as a means to develop a full rhythmic swing where tension and relaxation act both as preparation and result.

CONTRACTIONS AND TILTS

Under this heading are classified—

(a) the position of the limbs and the torso each in relation to their own central line and

(b) the position of the torso in relation to the limbs and line of support.

CONTRACTIONS

The major contractions occur in the torso but can affect the arms and legs through the shoulder and the hip. Briefly, a contraction is a shortening of torso or limbs towards a central point, to form a strong concave arc.

Example :

By a contraction in the torso, round the spine, pull the shoulders forward and downwards, and tip the pelvis backwards and under. At the same time, lift and shorten the arm by rotating inwards at the shoulder and contracting the biceps.

(73) *Forward Contraction.*

This contraction is taken about the vertical line of balance, towards the centre of the body.

Contractions can also be taken sideways, backwards and diagonally.

(74)
Sideways Contraction.
Taken about a vertical
line towards a centre
point of one side.

In the case of the backwards contraction, the spine is really in hyper-extension but the effect is that of a contraction.

Contractions are always brought about by tension towards the centre point on the inside of the arc of the movement and accompanied by a rounding of the spine or limb on the outside.

Many variations of steps, jumps, and supports can be taken as the basis of a contraction and transitions made from one contraction to another, as long as the major contraction in the body is maintained.

(75)

Backwards Contraction. Taken about a vertical line towards a centre point of the spine.

(76)

Diagonal Contraction. Taken about a diagonal line towards a point at side centre.

TILTS

Tilts are mainly of two kinds.

(*a*) Fixed : That in which the trunk and limbs are equally balanced on either side of the line of support (like a see-saw), and

(*b*) Flexible : In which trunk and limbs fall away freely from the line of support on the same side.

Examples—(*a*) Fixed Tilts.

(77) *Fixed Tilt Forwards.*   (78) *Fixed Tilt Sideways.*

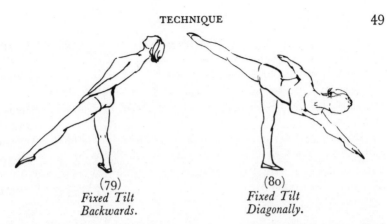

(79)
*Fixed Tilt
Backwards.*

(80)
*Fixed Tilt
Diagonally.*

In all cases of Fixed Tilts, there must be enough controlled tension to maintain the line through the centre point of balance.

(*b*) Flexible Tilts.

(81)
*Flexible Tilt
Forwards.*

(82) *Flexible Tilt
Backwards.*

(83) *Flexible Tilt
Sideways.*

(84) *Flexible Tilt
Diagonally.*

In all cases of Flexible Tilts, there must be enough relaxation to enable the trunk and limbs to flow out freely from the centre point of support along their own line.

Tilts may be taken at all Support Levels and combined with steps and jumps, also variations of transition from one to another can be used.

In studying Contractions and Tilts many variations between arms, legs and torso can be found, but each tilt or contraction will contain its own expression according to its direction, and placing in the body.

TURNS

A turn is basically a change of direction in which the body rotates round a vertical centre line. This can be done by spinning round with very fast changes of weight from foot to foot, but for purposes of Dance Classification a Turn is considered to be supported on one leg only, or taken whilst in the air with no support. Any divergence from this designation would be specially described, i.e., a half or quarter turn on both feet, is frequently referred to not as a turn but as a change of front.

Turns fall into two main categories—Stable and Labile.

STABLE TURNS

In these turns the weight is placed vertically over the support throughout, allowing the turn to be stopped at any moment without changing the body position. Changes of body position can be made during a turn, but the weight must always be in the vertical line of support whilst doing so. Support levels may also be changed throughout a turn.

Examples :

(85)   (86)   (87)

Deep to high Stable Turn inwards.

(88)   (89)   (90)

High to deep Stable Turn outwards.

The use of outwards and inwards (corresponding to the Classical terms en dehors and en dedans) refer to the direction of the turn in relation to the supporting leg. When the hip on the supporting side goes backwards and that on the gesture side goes forward, the turn is inwards (or dedans) whatever the line of body or leg and whether stable or labile. When the hip on the supporting side comes forward and that on the gesture side goes backwards, the turn is outwards (or dehors).

USE OF THE HEAD

In both stable and labile turns, the head can be used as an extension of the neck with no fixed eye focus, or it may be used as a separate limb and turned independently on the neck as in Classical Ballet " spotting ". Variations in the use of the head will affect the expression of the turns.

In all Stable Turns there must be enough controlled tension to maintain the correct placing of weight.

LABILE TURNS

In these Turns the weight is carried beyond the centre line of support on a diagonal line and can only be maintained while the body is in motion. In order to stop a Labile Turn, the movement must be stabilised, or another labile turn taken on the other foot. A labile turn can be stabilised by bringing the weight vertically over the support on a step, by following a labile turn with a stable turn, or by changing the body position whilst turning.

Examples :

(91)
*Labile Turn
inwards.*

(92)
*Labile Turn
outwards.*

(93)
*Labile Turn
stabilised by step.*

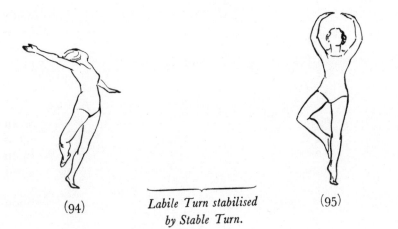

(94)   *Labile Turn stabilised*   (95)
            by Stable Turn.

In all Labile Turns there must be enough relaxation to enable the body to swing outside its vertical line of support from a fixed central point of control.

Both Stable and Labile Turns can be co-ordinated with steps and jumps by which to travel across the floor.

FALLS

Falls are classified here according to their fundamental nature, and are not described in terms of the detailed placing of the body in order to achieve a Stage Fall for dramatic effect. There are two mains ways in which any part or the whole of the body and limbs can fall. These are called Inside and Outside Falls.

INSIDE FALLS

A complete inside fall is one in which the body collapses upon the floor from an upright position, falling downwards in the line of gravity until the body rolls over outside the area of supports and spreads itself on the floor.

Examples :

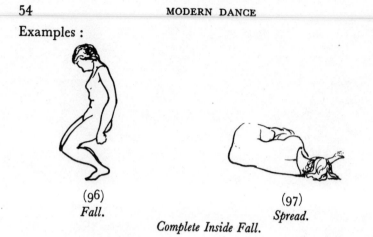

(96)
Fall.

(97)
Spread.

Complete Inside Fall.

This can be taken partially, where the body sags downwards, but is still supported by the hips and legs, or where the body is upright but the hips and legs have fallen on to the knees.

(98)

(99)

Partial Inside Fall.

In all cases of inside falls of the body and legs, the centre of gravity gives way, causing the pelvis to tip. An inside fall must therefore start in the pelvis.

Arms. An inside fall of the arm is one where the whole arm collapses from an upright position and falls to the side, in the line of gravity.

In the upright position the arm is supported by the shoulder, therefore in an Inside Fall the shoulder must give way first, allowing the rest of the arm to fall towards it.

All Inside Falls start by collapsing within the area of their support.

OUTSIDE FALLS

These are caused by allowing, or forcing the body or limbs, to move outside the area of support. There will be no collapsing in this case, but the fall of the body or limb will be in one piece.

Examples :

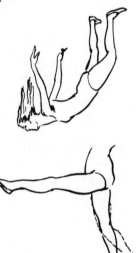

(100)
Complete Outside Fall from a height.

(101)
Outside Fall of Leg from the hip.

In the case of Arms and Legs, falls can be allowed to complete themselves, or be carried over as an impetus for a following movement. A complete inside fall of the body results in a collapse to the floor, but a complete outside fall must be caught on a support before it reaches the floor, or used as the impetus for the following movement. A complete outside fall of the body that is not caught or carried forward occurs only when diving or falling from a height.

Examples :

(102)
*Fall halted by a step
into support.*

(103)
*Fall impetus carried
forwards on a run.*

(104)

Falls of both kinds must be studied in all parts of the body as they are an essential part of economy of effort, and the basis of swings and impulses.

SWING

The Natural Swing is the Pendulum, the principle of which lies at the root of all swings. Its use in Dance Training is to achieve the fullest extension of movement by the most economical means.

Example :

(105)
Raising and lowering the arms with no swinging impetus.

The downward and upward movements have no connection with each other and could be stopped at any moment as there is always a control of tension present in the movement.

(106)

The same with a Pendulum swing.

The arms are now dropped by an outside fall, gaining weight as they near the extremity of the fall. The impetus carries them on beyond the vertical line. From here they fall again, adding a second impetus to the initial fall. This carries them forward and upward above the horizontal line. The arms are thus achieving a fuller extension of movement. It is not so easy to stop this arm movement as in the example shown in Fig. 106 because the work is done by gravity and not by the use of tension.

The principle of the outside fall and pick up of a Pendulum Swing can be used in isolated leg and trunk movements, and can also be co-ordinated throughout the whole body.

Examples :

(107)

Pendulum
Leg Swing.

(108)

Pendulum
Trunk Swing.

(109)
*Co-ordinated
Swing.*

As in a mechanical pendulum, the swinging body must be related to a fixed point. In using swing, therefore, as a means of achieving economy of effort and extension of movement, there must be a fixed point of control from which the movement stems. In the case of arms and legs, this fixed point is at shoulder and hips. In a co-ordinated swing affecting the whole body, the fixed point of control is in the centre of the body which must be placed firmly over the supporting leg.

In the above examples it will be seen that the rise of the swing is the result of the fall, and because of this, Swings of arms, legs and trunk can be used as aids to jumps and turns.

Example :

(110)   (111)   (112)
Arched jump on a swing.

(113)   (114)   (115)

(116)   (117)

A co-ordinated side swing with turn into long kneel, back swing and rise.

In this sequence, the motive power is swing throughout.

Fig. 113. Body and arm fall while leg rises in a co-ordinated swing.

Fig. 114. The trunk is turned on the upswing, the heel rising on the impetus.

Fig. 115. The arms continue a full circle backwards while the leg falls downwards to support the forward moving pelvis.

Fig. 116. The trunk swings forward and the arms complete a circle forward.

Fig. 117. Trunk, arms and the back leg swing forward and upward to lift the body on to the supporting toe.

Many other jumps and turns are possible by the practice of Swing.

CENTRIFUGAL SWING

The Pendulum swing gains its impetus by means of a fall towards gravity from a fixed point and therefore operates in a vertical line. Swings can be forward and back, side to side or diagonally forward and back, but they will always pass the centre line of the body as they are falling.

A Centrifugal Swing is basically one that has its impetus supplied by a fling outwards from the centre line of the body, and maintains a smooth motion in a horizontal plane. In this case the swing encircles the centre line of the body.

Examples :

(118)
Spinning round with small steps with outflung arms.

(119)
Hopping turn on one leg with centrifugal swing.

(120)
Turn on one leg with centrifugal arm and leg swing.

Centrifugal action can be used in other planes to extend the area of a pendulum swing. A full circling of the arms vertically can aid a jump and assist body mobility.

By combining Pendulum Swings and Centrifugal Swings ; a rising and falling from a point ; circling round a point ; and revolving about a centre line, many variations of co-ordination, leaps and turns can be made.

Example :

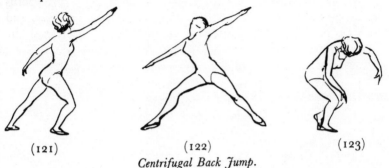

(121) (122) (123)

Centrifugal Back Jump.

In all the above examples of Pendulum and Centrifugal Swing, the impetus supplied by gravity and centrifugal force make for economy of effort and wide extension of movement, but must be brought under control by a fixed point or line of control at the centre. Placing of weight in relation to the base therefore is important.

THE EIGHT SWING

The Eight Swing is so called because it follows a figure of 8 design and thereby achieves maximum range in one uninterrupted movement which swings from a clockwise circle into a counter-clockwise circle.

Examples :

(124) (125) (126)

8 swing of the right arm.

The right arm drops into a pendulum swing across the front of the body, and rises in front and over the head and out to sideways high in a clockwise circle (124). From here it drops without pause into a pendulum swing behind the body (125) rising behind and over the head and out to sideways high in a counter-clock circle (126). From here the swing is continued as before.

By the nature of the shoulder joint the range of movement is from side to side, from high to deep and from forward to backward. This gives the swing a diagonal plane of movement and involves inward and outward rotation of the joint.

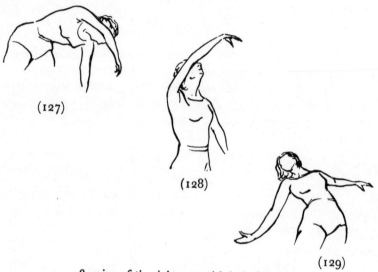

(127)

(128)

(129)

8 swing of the right arm with body following.

In this example the movement of the arm is allowed to come through the shoulders to the spine and down to the pelvis. Thus the whole spine swings in a diagonal plane, moving from side to side, from high to deep and from forwards to backward and involves an inward sinking and outward expansion of the body. This is made possible by the power of bending, stretching and rotating in the spine.

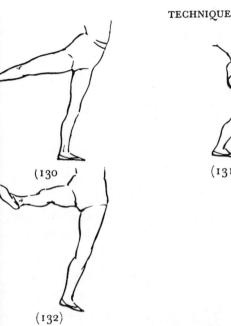
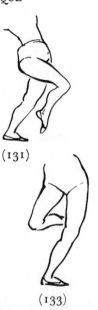

(130)

(131)

(132)

(133)

8 swing of the leg.

The leg swing follows the same principle as the arm, but has less range of movement. The swing occurs in front and behind the supporting leg in a continuous rising and falling action accompanied by inward and outward rotation of the hip joint. The rise and fall of the swinging leg necessitates a bending and stretching of the supporting leg on each swing. One complete swing therefore is accompanied by bending and stretching twice on the supporting leg.

Many combinations of eight swings of arm and leg with co-ordinated or counter movements can be found, and as with Pendulum and Centrifugal Swings, Steps, Jumps and Turns may easily be combined.

INVERTED SWINGS

The foregoing swings have made use of the impetus of fall in order to rise. These are all based on the Pendulum Principle. By inverting the Principle and rising in order to fall, a regular swing is obtained on the principle of a metronome.

Diagram 5

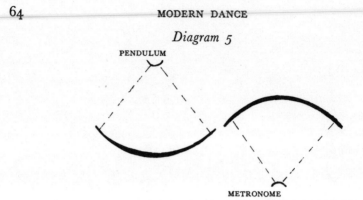

A combination of the Swing and the Inverted Swing will result in a complete circle with accent either at the top or bottom.

IMPULSES

Any part of the body, arms and legs can move on an impulsive rhythm, or over an impulsive phrase, but under the above classification certain key body movements are grouped. A body impulse starts in the pelvis with a downward fall to gather impetus. Strength is quickly gathered and thrust explosively forward and upward. As the energy is expended the pelvis is allowed to rise to its original position from where it starts its fall once again. Thus with continued forward impulses the pelvis moves in a backwards–downwards–forwards–upwards–circle with an accent at the bottom of the circle.

Example :

(134) (135) (136)   (137)
Preparation. *Fall. Forward Thrust. Return to original position.*

FORWARD IMPULSE

The wave of energy thus thrust outwards from the pelvis can be allowed to flow up through the spine and head, outwards along the shoulders and arms and downwards through the legs to the feet. This necessitates a relaxed and mobile spine. As the thrust of energy travels down into the feet, the resistance of the floor will be felt by a sharp pressure of the balls of the feet. This gives added force to the forward and upward thrust of the pelvis, and will pull the heels up off the floor. They will sink again to the floor as the pelvis returns to normal and rise again in preparation for the next drop and thrust.

In the full body impulse, the arms are raised in preparation to aid the fall. They, with the trunk and head, fall forward as the pelvis drops. This gives the slight tilt to the pelvis as it falls, in preparation for the forward and upward thrust.

Basically the above movement will be seen to be a backward-forward circling of the pelvis with a strong accent at the bottom of the circle. The rest of the body follows through.

This circling of the pelvis can be made in the opposite direction. This results in a back impulse.

BACK IMPULSE

In this movement the same principle of fall, thrust and follow through is maintained, but the pelvis drops downward and forward, gathers impetus, and thrusts backwards and upwards. As in the forward impulse the arms and torso fall to aid impetus. Since the fall is backwards, the heels are pulled up immediately and lowered on the thrust.

Example :

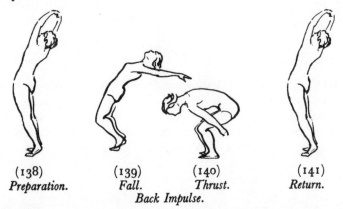

(138)   (139)   (140)   (141)
Preparation.   *Fall.*   *Thrust.*   *Return.*
Back Impulse.

Basically this movement is a forward-backward circling of the pelvis with a strong accent at the bottom of the circle.

SIDE IMPULSE

The side impulse follows the same pattern and rhythm as the Forward and Back, but is taken to the left or right.

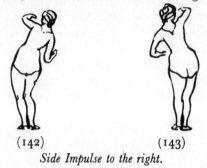

(142)   (143)

Side Impulse to the right.

The Pelvis tips downwards to the right as the Trunk and Arm fall downward and inwards to the right. From here it is thrust strongly to the right and upwards on its return to normal. Thus the pelvis circles in a counter-clockwise direction with a strong accent at the bottom of the circle. The heels are pulled up at the moment of thrust and sink to the floor as the pelvis returns to normal.

In taking impulses with arms only, legs only or head only, the same principle of fall, thrust and follow through is kept. The movement starts at the shoulder, hips or neck and flows out through the limb. The study of impulse gives valuable training in relaxation and rhythmic vitality.

Impulses can be combined with Transference of Weight Steps, Jumps and Turns, and many variations can be found.

FLOW

In the Section on Principles of Movement examples were given of movements that were by nature free flowing, and others that were by nature guided. In dance movement, the natural flow can be allowed to follow out its path, or a guidance of tension can be present to control the movement at every moment. The terms Free Flow and Bound Flow are used to indicate this difference.

Examples :

The arms and head are tossed outwards and allowed to fall back to normal as the initial impulse is expended.

(144)
Arms moving with Free Flow.

In this example, the position has been reached steadily and can be maintained at any point.

(145)
Bound Flow Movement.

In a dance Technique the natural flow of movement is constantly being freed or bound, and the dancer must experience this by practising many movements of each kind.

In Dance Studies based on Free and Bound Flow, it is possible to have sustained passages of smooth controlled movement followed by the quick freeing of the controlling tension. The term Guided is convenient for describing any lengthy use of Bound Flow to differentiate from the periodic binding of the flow in passing from one free movement to another. A study based on Free Flow entirely would be lacking in shape and purpose, whilst one based on Bound Flow only would be over formal and lacking in warmth and rhythmic vitality. There must be a natural rise and fall to enliven the smooth sustained control, and a periodic catching up of control to clarify and organise spontaneous freedom.

In this example the first movement takes 4 counts to do. The weight is transferred slowly and smoothly to the side, while the arm and trunk reach their line. There is a light control of tension throughout. On " and " the tension is released into a fall. The impetus is caught up into a change of direction and level. Body, head and arms are tossed upwards on the impulse from the pelvis, heels are drawn up from the floor and a moment of poise is reached as the upward impulse flows on. As the natural fall downwards is about to occur, control is taken over again with light tension and a slow transference of weight with a hand and arm gesture is made over " 2 and 3 ". Control is again released in an upward change of weight on to the back leg and the whole movement falls forward and downward to the floor.

It will be noticed that in the Bound Flow movements " 1–4 " and " 2–3 " there is a sustainment of control that could bring the movement to a standstill at any moment, whilst on the Free Flow movements " and 1 " " and 4 " there is a following through of initial impetus which expends itself naturally and can only be stopped by added effort.

It can be seen also that the direction of the first Bound Flow movement " 1–4 " is upward and is followed by a natural fall downward " and ". This becomes a Free Flow movement upwards " 1 " which is followed by a Bound Flow movement downwards " 2–3 ". The next " and " is a release of control which is caught up into an upward impetus followed by a natural fall " 4 ".

This Sequence must be danced rhythmically and with clarity of line. If it is danced with Bound Flow throughout, it will lose its rhythmic quality which should be like a " breath " contained within its shape. It would be impossible to dance this sequence with Free Flow throughout as " 1–4 " and " 2–3 " could not be sustained.

Examples :

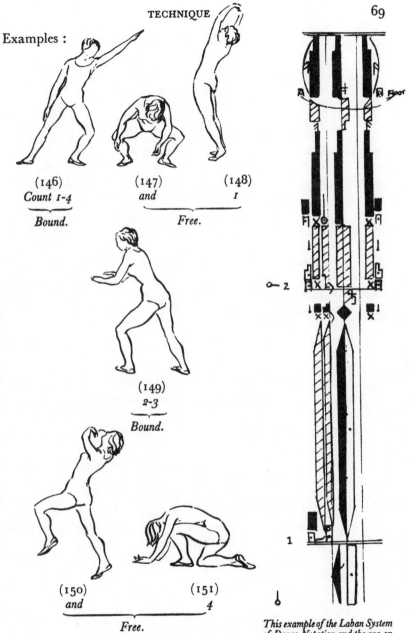

(146)
Count 1-4
Bound.

(147)
and

(148)
1

Free.

(149)
2-3
Bound.

(150)
and

(151)
4

Free.

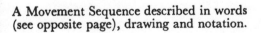

A Movement Sequence described in words (see opposite page), drawing and notation.

This example of the Laban System of Dance Notation and the one on page 69 were notated by Edna Geer by arrangement with the British Dance Notation Society.

This sequence follows exactly the same directions as the one in Fig. 113, but the nature of the Flow has been reversed.

The transference of weight to the side is taken with Free Flow on "and 1". Notice that the clarity of line has gone, being replaced by a softer outline. The downward and upward movement with a change of direction is now done with Bound Flow " 2, 3, 4 ". Notice the three clear-cut positions which indicate a smooth transition from one to the other making one sustained movement. The transference of weight with hand and arm gesture now becomes a Free Flow fall on to the front foot " and ". The last change of weight on to the back leg followed by a fall on to the front leg is now done with Bound Flow, and becomes a gesture with slow weight transference " 1–4 ".

Comparison of these two examples will show how the shape and speed are affected by the nature of the Flow and how Free and Bound Flow, Tension and Relaxation, Weight and Strength and the three Basic Rhythms (Principles of Movement Section) are all concerned in the execution of both sequences.

ADAGE

This word used as a noun is derived from the musical term " ad-agio," an Italian expression meaning at ease—comfortably— at a slow pace.

An Adage in dancing is a sequence of movements following one another slowly and smoothly in perfect equilibrium. This necessitates the weight being supported on one leg while slowly unfolding gestures are taking place. This will prove to be anything but " comfortable and at ease " unless the dancer has already studied and practised balance, co-ordination and economy of effort. These principles run throughout the whole of the foregoing chapters and must be the core of dance training.

BALANCE

The ability to stand on one leg is possessed by everyone who can walk, but not everyone can sustain this moment of single

(152)
(fall) and

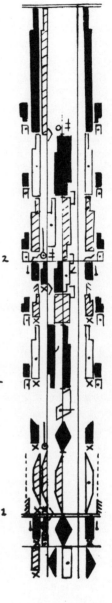

(153)
I

Free.

(154)   (155)   (156)
2   3   4

Bound.

(157)
(fall) and Free.

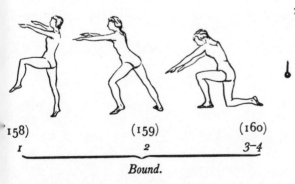

158)   (159)   (160)
I   2   3-4

Bound.

See note on page 69.

The same sequence as on page 69 with
a different flow.

support.　This is because the manner of one's walking is determined by where the weight is placed in relation to the supports. The centre of gravity is where we are aware of the weight of the body.　If the spine is in correct alignment with the pelvis and the whole body is in alignment over the feet, the resulting posture will be balanced and economical, avoiding strain from over tight or over slack muscles.

(161)　　　　　　　　(162)　　　　　　　　(163)

Correct alignment　　*Muscles too tight.*　　*Muscles too slack.*

Good posture.　　　*Bad posture.*　　　*Bad posture.*

Good posture is essential to every dancer as from this stems all the line and flow of movement.　From the correct alignment of the body comes a balance of limbs on either side of the vertical centre line.　Unless the limbs are considered in relation to the centre line and the body in relation to the centre point, the whole will resemble only so many sticks in a bundle indiscriminately tied together.

(164)　　　　　　　　　　　　　(165)

Balanced　　　　　　　　　　*Unbalanced*

line.　　　　　　　　　　　*line.*

The sustained balance of Adage is achieved by daily practice of good posture and alignment in all dance technique and in the co-ordination of one part of the body with another.

CO-ORDINATION

The verb—to co-ordinate—means " to bring the parts of a system into proper relation " In " the system " of the working of the body, the parts of the body are brought into proper relation by their connection with the centre point or line of the whole. Co-ordination and Balance therefore, are inseparable.   Unless there is a co-ordination of movement through the centre, there can be no Balance of line or Postural alignment.   Co-ordination of movement through the centre is essential to every dancer in order to find the harmony of a balanced line in respose.

(166)
A Co-ordinated jump.

(167)
An Unco-ordinated jump.

The slowly forming line and design of an Adage is brought to a perfection of harmony by the co-ordination of movement through the centre and sustained by the balance of good postural alignment.   The combination of Balance and Co-ordination gives to the Adage its calm undisturbed beauty, where hard work, effort and strain are not apparent.   Economy of effort is the result of this partnership and is the third factor which is essential to a dancer.

ECONOMY OF EFFORT

The term effort unfortunately is too often connected with undue strain. Tension is another word which suggests to many an unnatural tautening of the nerves and muscles, while Relaxation is frequently interpreted as a total sag. The dancer must learn to understand both these terms as the names for active forces at work in the body, and by constant practice, learn to use them in accordance with her own needs. Tension and Relaxation have already been discussed in Principles of Movement and in connection with Flow.

It is common knowledge that the body is kept upright by the balancing of one muscle group against another, and that whenever a movement is made, one muscle pulls and another gives. All muscles have the power of pulling, giving or just holding, and the balance of these three functions makes possible the complex movements of the body and limbs. The dancer must know when and where to pull, when and where to give, when and where to hold. The daily practice enables her to achieve an " understanding " body. Knowledge of her technique and an understanding of Principles of Movement are necessary to intelligent practice, but the " understanding " or " feel " of the movement in the body is the aim of that practice, in order to achieve economy of effort. Too much tension will produce a hard line and an unsympathetic flow of movement. Not only will it cause strain to the dancer but will exhaust and even antagonise an audience. Too much relaxation will produce a sloppy line and a sentimental or over emotional flow of movement. Over relaxation causes strain on the parts of the body that take the weight and a constantly sagging dancer will cause distaste and embarrassment to an audience.

Economy of effort balances out Tension and Relaxation by rhythmic timing. All dance practice must be rhythmic. An unrhythmic movement is lacking in economy of effort and so induces fatigue and strain. The dancer's daily lesson must always be taken on a rhythmic basis in order that she may learn the " feel " of every movement in relation to the centre as well as the placing of the weight over the centre of support and the alignment of her limbs to a centre line.

The metrical counting of the duration of a movement must not be confused with the awareness of its rhythmical flow. It is possible to be metrically faithful to a beat and remain entirely rhythmically unaware. Although a rhythmic movement can fit easily into a time beat, rhythm itself stems from the right relationship of all parts to the whole rather than from the mathematical regimentation of the whole.

Adage is the supreme achievement of balance, co-ordination and economy of effort and the reward to the dancer for intelligent and understanding practice.

Design and feeling are perfectly balanced in Adage when the dancer's technique has been digested with rhythmic understanding. Then the dancer and audience can move along together " comfortably—at a slow pace—and at ease ".

THE TRAINING CLASS

The training of a Modern Dancer to-day is broader than that of a Classical Dancer in so far as it sets out to produce not only a dancer, a teacher and a choreographer, but also an individual. Teachers and choreographers may emerge from any method of training, but the special aim of Modern Dance is to develop the personality of each dancer through the training, by creative improvisation and composition. This means more than an ability to put steps together from a limited vocabulary, and necessitates a deeper knowledge of the underlying rules of dynamics and design than the Technical Class gives. It is necessary, therefore, as part of a Modern Dancer's training, for her to have regular classes in Dynamics and Design, Improvisation and Composition, in addition to the daily Technique Class. For purposes of clarity, Technique is here considered to be concerned only with what the body can do anatomically, together with the operation of the Principles of Movement in the body. Dynamics and Design are, of course, inseparable from Technique, but in training are separated for purposes of special study. These will be dealt with in separate Sections.

GENERAL FORM OF THE DAILY TECHNICAL
TRAINING CLASS

This follows broadly the same form as a Classical Class. The dancer does her barre, follows with centre practice, and then is lead into a Movement Sequence or Study.

Training Studies are an important part of Modern Dance, as they give the dancer a progressive framework within which to work for herself, and provide a convenient and stimulating means for concentration upon one or another of the Technical Themes.

The teacher selects a theme for the class according to the needs and ability of his students. This theme is adhered to throughout the whole class, and every barre exercise and centre practice is taken in relation to it. For example—if the theme for the lesson is Free and Bound Flow, barre and centre will be arranged so that Free and Bound Flow exercises will follow one another, in short phrases, and long ones ; in one part of the body and another. By this means the body is being prepared for its special study whilst undergoing its daily routine. This gives the teacher scope for creative teaching and keeps the barre and centre alive rather than automatic. Perhaps the theme will be a less fluid one, like Basic Steps. In this case, a barre and a centre practice must be built up on Support, Gesture and Transference of Weight, and this must be the basis of the Study to be worked on.

By means of Training Studies on selected Themes, the teacher can compose as he goes along and thereby work progressively with his students. He can accommodate the Study to any special difficulties of his class whilst teaching the fundamental principle contained in the theme, and can thus demand maximum concentration whilst giving great variety.

In the daily Technical Training Class the Study is led up to through the barre and centre practice, and then is taken phrase by phrase, either coming down the room or across the diagonal. The phrases are broken up into fundamentals as necessary, either in the centre, or travelling down the room, and these are built up gradually into small movement phrases and repeated many times until they are kinaesthetically digested. The next phrase is taken in the same way, by building up from fundamentals as before. When the class is nearing its end, the phrases are danced together many times, and part of a study is then ready for each dancer to work at in her own practice time. The next day the study will be continued by the same means, and so a progressive sequence is learned from day to day. By progressing from theme to theme by means of Studies, a training is slowly built up on fundamentals of movement.

THE BARRE

Exercises at the barre should be done daily in the same order, although variations and combinations should be made. It is of great importance that each exercise be done slowly and carefully in order to feel the correct placing of weight over the supports, the steady rhythmic flow, and the co-ordination and alignment of the whole body to the moving part.

Posture at the Barre is of the utmost importance as the foundation of equilibrium and economy of movement is laid here. Faults made regularly at the Barre are not only difficult to put right in the centre, but will probably cause other faults to occur in order to compensate for bad posture and alignment.

The Barre must neither be hung on nor pressed upon, and at any moment the dancer should be able to remove her hand without undue wriggling to find her balance. The Barre should be used as an aid to find one's equilibrium rather than as a substitute for it.

The inclusion of some fundamentals of Classical Ballet is inescapable. In their simplest form, all dance methods stem from the same root. The simple Classical Barre, therefore, is used as the basis for the Modern Barre, and terms and practices which are established have been kept.

The essence of Modern Dance, however, is its creative potentiality and its dynamic content, and it is therefore necessary to know more of the elements from which a very wide range of expressive movements issue.

A recorded method or technical syllabus must only serve as a disciplinary framework within which to create every shade of expression possible to the individual dancer or teacher. The study of the varying qualities of movement in which expression lies, is the subject of the next section.

SUMMARY [1]

In the foregoing section we have been mostly concerned with the anatomical and simple rhythmic possibilities of the body. Briefly, the body can bend, stretch and rotate. In doing so the joints and muscles can combine together to produce three different rhythmic accents.

Initial Accent ♩ ♪ :   Impulsive

Transitional Accent ♪ ♩ ♪ : Swinging

Terminal Accent ♪ ♩ :   Purposeful

Each type of rhythm can be classified in terms of flow.
  Impulsive : The freeing of Flow
  Swinging :   From freeing to binding of Flow
  Purposeful : The binding of Flow

Each type of rhythm can be classified in terms of Tension and Relaxation :

  Impulsive : Expending of Tension

  Swinging :   Passing from Relaxation to Tension and again
               to Relaxation

  Purposcful : Gathering of Tension.

Lastly, weight can be transferred and moved into any direction.

On the above simple basic facts, a dance technique can be built as a foundation for training. Since a technique must always impose a style and therefore a limitation, a great number of set exercises have not been laid down. If the fundamentals are understood and built upon, the teacher and dancer are limited less than by following copious directions. The foregoing classification and examples are intended only as a guide and should be used by the individual in her own way.

[1] See Author's Note, page 6.

CHAPTER III

DYNAMICS [1]

THE quality of movement in dancing is like colour in painting and harmonies in music. While line and design can delight the eye and move one to aesthetic appreciation, it is the dynamic quality in dancing that speaks to the emotions and conveys the human content of the movement. To develop quality in Dance Training, it is necessary to understand and experience the elements from which it springs. There are three fundamental elements to be considered in movement.

Energy.   Design.   Speed.

As with the primary colours, Red, Blue and Yellow, these elements have so many gradations that they cannot be spoken of as constants, but are referred to in terms of the two extremes between which each element moves.

ENERGY

Energy is referred to, in terms of growing tension which becomes as strong as possible with a maximum of resistance, and of increasing relaxation which becomes as heavy as possible with a minimum of resistance. A movement is described as Strong or Light, Heavy or Soft according to the degree of Tension or Relaxation it contains. In everyday life we delegate varying degrees of strength or weight to specific areas in the body and for special skills or crafts, develop the particular group of muscles concerned with the activity.

Example :

(168)   (169)

Using the finger ends for   *Using the heel of the*
lightness in pastry making. *hand for kneeding clay.*

[1] See Author's Note, page 6.

For the dancer, however, the body is more than a functional machine, and must be trained to move any part of the body with the strength or lightness that is characteristic of another part. From inert heaviness to a floating activity, there is a span of innumerable degrees of energy, and in classifying movements in terms of strength and weight, it must be understood that for the dancer, relaxation must be a consciously practised quality, which can contain as many shades. Practices in degrees and shades of Strength and Weight must be part of her daily training.

For purposes of clarity, the element of Energy in movement is therefore referred to as *Strong or Light* (*tension*) *Heavy or Soft* (*relaxation*).

DESIGN

The design of body movement is dependent upon the situation of the starting point of movement, and the order in which joints connected with the movement go into action. In studying the design of movement as a basic element, we are only concerned with the relationship of the origin of the movement to the centre of the body.

A Central movement is one which originates either in the centre of the body, or at a joint in a limb which is connected to the body.

Example :

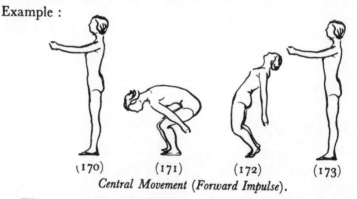

(170)   (171)   (172)   (173)

Central Movement (Forward Impulse).

The movement originates in the centre of the body and flows outwards. Continuous impulses will all originate at the body centre.

(174)

Central Arm Movement.

In this example, the arm has been lifted up as a result of the activity in the shoulder girdle and rib cage.

(175)   (176)

Central Leg Movements.

The leg is being drawn along the ground on the heel and then on the toe continuously. The foot in each case follows passively through as the movement starts each time in the pelvis.

Heads, hands and feet can move with a central expression and small subtleties can be conveyed in any part of the body by Central means. Wherever they occur and whatever area they cover, Central movements start their activity at a point near to the main part of the limb or at the junction of the limb with the trunk. In working outwards from this central starting point, the design of the movement is undulating.

A Peripheral movement is one in which the activity starts at the extremities of a limb or at a point farthest away from the centre of the body.

MD—6

The head is turned upon its axis without disturbing the neck.

(177)
Peripheral Head Movement.

The hands and arms have been lifted without disturbing the shoulder girdle.

(178)
Peripheral Arm Movement.

The knee has been lifted without disturbing the pelvis. A certain lateral pelvic shifting is necessitated by the transference of weight from double to single support, but this is not a result of the movement in the leg.

(179)
Peripheral Leg Movement.

The Trunk has been turned as a whole without disturbing the centre.

(180)
Peripheral Body Movement.

In all examples of Peripheral movements, there is a characteristic directness, and the design is an undeviating one.

In daily practices of Central and Peripheral movements, the dancer will become aware of the rhythmic flow between these two designs. The natural development of a Central movement in Dance Technique is to become Peripheral as a completely central sphere of movements would be too personal. A Peripheral sphere of movement only would become too stilted. The natural development of a Peripheral movement is to involve the centre and draw it into the line of action. The dancer's practice will cover the many relationships possible between these two fundamental elements of design, which in the study of dynamics are classified as *Central and Peripheral*.

SPEED

The third element to be considered is the gathering and losing of speed. As it flows away from the centre, movement loses speed and gains it when flowing in towards the centre. It is only possible to maintain a constant speed in locomotion across the floor or in movements that do not pass through the centre of the body. To move at a constant speed indefinitely is very harmful as it destroys the natural rhythm, and a dancer who constantly moves too suddenly or too tardily is subjecting herself to unnecessary strain. The motivation of a movement will determine whether the natural rhythm is a sudden or a sustained action, and in the dancer's training there must be many variations in the flow of speed. For purposes of classification, these are referred to as *Quick and Slow*.

SUMMARY OF THE ELEMENTS [1]

Basic elements of movement. Energy. Design. Speed.

Energy :	Strong Light (Tension).	Heavy Soft (Relaxation).
Design.	Central (Undulating).	Peripheral (Undeviating).
Spced :	Quick (Sudden).	Slow (Sustained).

[1] See Author's Note, page 6.

THE EIGHT FUNDAMENTAL QUALITIES

In analysing movement in terms of these three elements it must be understood that they are bound up together and inter-dependent. A change in one element will affect the other two. The essential importance of one element in relation to another will vary according to the type of movement and the conditions under which it is performed. It is, however, possible to make eight basic combinations of these fundamental element changes. These form the foundations of all shades of dance expression.

Diagram 6

	STRONG	LIGHT	CENTRAL	PERIPHERAL	QUICK	SLOW
1	●		●			●
2		⌂		⌂	⌂	
3	▄			▄		▄
4		⌀	⌀		⌀	
5	●		●		●	
6		⌐		⌐		⌐
7	◣			◣	◣	
8		●	●			●

The symbols indicate as follows.

Filled in = Strong	Circle = Central	Tail up = Quick
Open = Light	Square = Peripheral	Tail down = Slow

1. Strong Central Slow ●   5. Strong Central Quick ●
2. Light Peripheral Quick ⌂   6. Light Peripheral Slow ⌐
3. Strong Peripheral Slow ▄   7. Strong Peripheral Quick ◣
4. Light Central Quick ⌀   8. Light Central Slow ●

[1] See Author's Note, page 6.

DEGREE OF ELEMENT CHANGE

In the early stages of a dancer's training Dynamic qualities should be practised in a very free way both in the body as a whole and in isolated parts of the body. Qualities may be studied separately or in relation to each other. It will be seen that each quality has one other which is an exact opposite in that each of the elements of movement contained in it are different.

Example :

    { Strong, Central, Slow.   **❯**

    { Light, Peripheral, Quick.   **◻**

    { Strong, Peripheral, Slow.   **◼**

    { Light, Central, Quick.   **6**

Working on qualities in pairs as above will give the dancer the greatest possible contrast in movement expression, but it is necessary also for her to be able to flow from one movement expression to another with a finer degree of sensitivity to change.

Example :

    { Strong, Central, Slow.   **❯**

    { Light, Central, Slow.   **9**

    { Light, Peripheral, Slow.   **⊐**

    { Light, Peripheral, Quick.   **◻**

In this example the dancer has moved through three transitional stages of movement expression and has come to the exact opposite in quality. Her change has not been abrupt and immediate as in the first example, but a harmonious shading from one to another.

From the following diagram it is possible to see how one of the basic combinations can lead to any one of the others, and whether the change is made by harmonious transition or with an immediate contrast.

Diagram 7

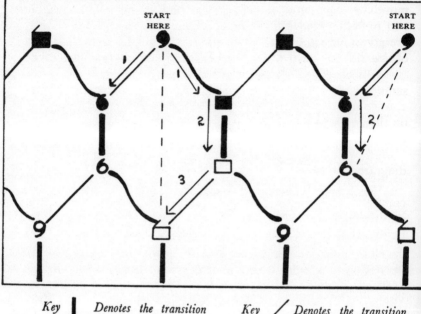

Key | *Denotes the transition by change of strength only.*   Key / *Denotes the transition by change of speed only.*

Key ⌇ *Denotes the transition by change of shape only.*

By starting at one of the symbols which indicate one of the eight basic combinations of elements, you can travel along a connecting line which will bring you to a different combination. This connecting line denotes the element which is changing to bring about a transition from one quality of expression to another.

For example : Start at the symbol indicated on the left of the Diagram and travel along the line marked I. By consulting the Keys to Diagram 6 and 7 you will see that your starting movement was a combination of a slow, a strong, and a central element, and your transition was by means of the element of speed. Your movement has now become quick, strong and central. These two qualities are similar in expression to a certain degree, but are given individuality by the difference in speed. A transition of this kind is called a one degree change.

A three-degree change is shown in diagram form from the same starting point. The three changes of element are numbered 1, 2, 3, but occur in one movement, so that the three paths shown on the diagram are by-passed in one abrupt change indicated by the dotted line.

A two-degree change is shown on the right of the diagram.

The teacher will find a very rich source from which to draw in composing dynamic movements of this nature, and the dancer's sensitivity to expressive changes contained in the sequences will be developed more and more fully.

In the early stages of free dynamic training, the many qualities of expression can be explored and brought to the surface by varied stimuli. These will be dealt with in the section on Improvisation and Composition. In later training, the teaching of expressive dynamic quality should be done within the framework of Technique.

For example :

This sissonne is a combination of the three elements, light- quick- and peripheral. It is sharp and direct in its attack, and is accompanied by clearly focused head movements from side to side. The arms and body are held in a light, straight tension, with no disturbance at the centre. The expression of this quality of sissonne is clear cut and sparkling.

(181) *A sissonne.*

In the second sissonne, the lightness and speed have remained, but the movement is done centrally. The expression now becomes softer and less directly focused. The body takes an active part with the head and arms giving the step a light-hearted charm.

(182)

A sissonne (**6**).

The pas de basque lends itself to many rhythmic and expressive variations. In the two shown below, the first is strong and vigorous, coming through the centre of the body, and the feet striking the ground with the whole weight of leg behind them. The dynamic quality is strong, quick, and central, and the expression that of a virile peasant. The contrasting pas de basque is light, slow, and peripheral. This is more suitable for a Court Dance with its smooth, controlled action and unhurried touch.

(183)   (184)

Peasant Pas de Basque (**6**).   *Court Pas de Basque* (**⊔**).

If the dancer is trained very fully and freely in dynamic changes of quality and expression, her Technique will be vitalised. Although Dynamics must be studied as a separate subject, it must, of course, finally be digested into the dancer's technical training. This is done by gradual transition from the study of movement elements, through the variations in the basic combinations of these, and finally on to specially composed studies where constantly changing dynamics within an ordered rhythm are taught through technical means.

SINGLE, SIMULTANEOUS AND DOUBLE TENSION [1]

Since the body can move as a whole or in isolated parts, it is possible to have more than one quality of movement happening at the same time. These can be classified under three main headings.

SINGLE TENSION

This term is used when all movements in the body made at the same time are of the same dynamic quality.

Example :

(185)

Head, Hand, Trunk and Step.

All Strong, Slow, Perpipheral.

SIMULTANEOUS TENSION

This term is used when two or more qualities of expression are present in different parts of the body.

Example :

(186)

Light Slow Peripheral. Strong Slow Central, Strong. Quick Peripheral.

The arms are drawn lightly and slowly upward as the trunk curls slowly and strongly backwards. Meanwhile the front heel raps quickly and strongly upon the floor.

[1] See Author's Note, page 6.

Many more variations of simultaneous tension can be found, and the study of rhythm and counter rhythm will be found to be valuable and stimulating.

DOUBLE TENSION

This term is used when two forces are active at the same time in the same part of the body. Every part can be moved from the centre or from the extremity. When Double Tension occurs in any quality, this means that there is a Central activity and a Peripheral activity operating in the same area of the body at the same time.

Example :

(187)
Double Tension.

In all movements containing Double Tension, the expression is one of conflict or lack of harmony.

SUMMARY

The study of dancing from a dynamic aspect necessitates an understanding of the expression contained in varying movement qualities arising from the following :

The Three Basic Elements :

Quality : Strong or Light.
Shape and Design : Central or Peripheral.
Speed : Quick or Slow.

The Eight Basic Combinations | Strong, Central, Slow.
resulting from the Three | Strong, Central, Quick.
Elements : | Strong, Peripheral, Slow.
| Strong, Peripheral, Quick.
| Light, Central, Slow.
| Light, Central, Quick.
| Light, Peripheral Slow.
| Light, Peripheral, Quick.

Degree of Element Change: Transition from one quality to another by changing 1, 2 or 3 elements.

Single, Simultaneous or Double | 1 quality of movement only.
Tension : | 2 or more qualities in different parts of the body.
| 3 Central and Peripheral activity in one part at the same time.

In training the dancer dynamically the teacher devises exercises, movement sequences, studies and dances which concentrate on changes of feeling and expression and draws upon the fundamentals classified here to give infinite variety. These basic classifications are, of course, the foundations for individual creative work, and when taken in combination with the practices in the Technique Section, a training is gradually built up to include the fullest dynamic range of expression within the widest possible rhythmic and anatomical use of the body.

So far, the dancer has worked from two aspects. Technically, to achieve range and control of movement through a flexible and well-placed body, and Dynamically to develop depth and sensitivity to the quality of expression in movement. The next things to be considered are clarity of shape and economy of design. A dancer with blurred outlines and a poor sense of design will finally also lack true dance expression, as she will succeed only in self-expression. Her own ability to feel the inner content and to move with feeling and expression will remain personal only unless she can organise it into a recognisable shape that will convey the content clearly. A study of the laws of harmony of Direction–and–Design is therefore included in the training of a Modern Dancer. This is dealt with in the next section.

CHAPTER IV

DIRECTION AND DESIGN [1]

The fundamental design of a movement, whether curved or straight, has already been referred to in the Technique and Dynamics sections. In this section the dancer is introduced to a detailed classification of the design of movement in the body and its direction in space. The sphere of bodily movement is defined as that within the body itself and also the area within reach of the dancer whilst keeping one foot stationary. As soon as the dancer carries her weight away from its support and transfers it to a completely new support, she is said to be moving in outer space as well as in the body. This moving in outer space is usually achieved by stepping, running, jumping, into any direction. There are, of course, other specialised ways of locomotion in outer space which need not be dealt with here.

The basis of the classification of bodily movement within itself and also in outer space, is that of the relation of the centre to the outside. Movement is either flowing from the centre outwards, or from the extremities to the centre. In order to make a design of straight lines in outer space, the body has to adjust its normal flow and co-ordinate centre with extremities. In the training of the dancer, this same adjustment has to be made. A truly naturally moving body would lack the specific clarity of line that is required in order for the dancer to be articulate. It becomes necessary, therefore, to classify the natural outflow and inflow of movement in stricter terms. For this purpose the three dimensions of all solid matter are used.

THE THREE DIMENSIONS

Starting from the body centre, and moving outwards, it is possible to classify six main directions, each one being the opposite of one other.

In the vertical line through the centre it is possible to go upwards or downwards.

In the horizontal line passing from side to side of the centre it is possible to open or close.

In the horizontal line passing from the front to back through the centre it is possible to advance or retreat.

[1] See Author's Note, page 6.

Anatomically the body is formed to move along these paths with special parts of the body.

The Trunk is mainly concerned with the rise and fall in the vertical line of gravity. The arms are arranged so that they may easily close in across the body or open sideways away from it, and the legs move in a forward and back direction in order to carry the body across the surrounding space. All parts of the body participate in the main action of another part, but in studying the design of the whole dance movement the essential part of the body or limb must be clearly defined.

Examples :

| (188)   (189) | (190) | (191) |
| *High Movements.* | *Deep Movements.* | |

High and Deep are the names given to the extremities of the vertical line of movement. This can be referred to as the First Dimension. In the examples shown here, the Trunk is rising to lightness in Figs. 188 and 189. In both cases the arms, head and legs are affected as the movement flows through the spine. Because of their own natural sphere of movement, the limbs do not move vertically up and down. The whole dance movement is classified as High, however, as the essential movement is in the Trunk.

Similarly in the two Deep movements, the legs and head moved forwards in order to go downwards, but the essence of the movement is in the sinking downwards of the Trunk. Both dance movements therefore are classified as Deep.

Narrow and Wide are the names given to the closing or opening of the arms in relation to the Trunk, along the horizontal line sideways. The arms are also capable of independent action and so movements can be made to one side only, or parallel. The legs are to a lesser degree concerned with opening and closing in relation to the centre, and in moving the arms and legs fully along this sideways line, the Trunk will naturally participate. A widening movement will tend to expand the Trunk and a narrowing movement will contract it. The legs in participating will tend to elongate on the wide movement and shorten on the narrowing, but the whole dance movement is classified as Wide or Narrow as the essential movement is in the arms and supported by the legs.

(192)   (193)
Wide.   *Narrow.*

Independent movements of arms or legs to one side or the other are referred to normally as right or left plus the classification wide or narrow.

(194)
Left Arm and Leg Wide.

This line of movement can be referred to as the Second Dimension.

The last two directions in relation to the centre are classified as Forward and Backward movements. These can be done with the arms and trunk, but a complete advance or retreat must be made by means of the legs.

(195)
Forward Movement.

(196)
Same with step.

In Fig. 195, the arms reach forward and the torso presses forward and outward in the rib cage, but the full feeling of a forward movement is not achieved unless a step or steps are made.

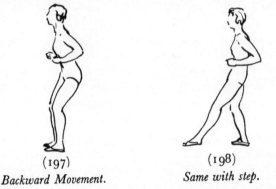

(197)
Backward Movement.

(198)
Same with step.

Similarly in the backward movement of the arms and torso, a direct line backwards is only achieved by the action of the legs. This line of movement can be referred to as the Third Dimension.

The six directions from the dancer's own body centre form the foundation of spatial balance and proportion, and provide her with a clearly cut pattern in space. Movement sequences can be composed upon these directions as tunes are composed upon the placing of notes in a scale. The dancer gradually becomes orientated to these basic directions and the parts of the body specially concerned with them. In acquiring the right muscular feel of the directions, she also becomes aware of the expressive significance contained in them, and in this way gains control of the medium through which her feelings can be communicated.

THE EXPRESSIVE SIGNIFICANCE OF THE THREE DIMENSIONS [1]

In the section of Dynamics, it was found that although the trained dancer aims to express any quality of feeling with any or every part of her body, certain actions and expressions are found by natural laws in specific areas of the body. This same principle is followed through in the expression inherent in the dimensional directions of body movements.

DIMENSION I.

This is the line on which gravity exercises its force, and is therefore connected with changes of weight or strength. Physically this means that movements going upwards get lighter and those going downwards get heavier. Since it is impossible to separate the several aspects of man into compartments, the emotional content of these movements follows the same pattern, and the dancer finds that physical lightness or heaviness cannot be divorced from emotional or spiritual activity of the same quality. Upwards movements then become those of release and downwards movements become those of bondage.

DIMENSION 2.

In the opening or closing movements of the arms about the body, and to a lesser degree the legs, there is a physical exposure or concealment of oneself. In the complete movement participation of the dancer, these become expressions of trust or doubt. If the movements of arms and legs are taken alternately to right or left, this creates a physical monotony which, if prolonged, can produce a deadly inertia. Movements to one side or another also contain an element of vacillation and of desire to escape, but these are more concerned with activity in the head and trunk.

[1] See Author's Note, page 6.

DIMENSION 3.

In the line of advance or retreat, the physical action is one of attack or defence, invitation or rejection, according to the surrounding conditions. Expressively this becomes translated into the feelings of sympathy or antipathy. These very basic expressions are found in their simplest form within the directional classification of the Three Dimensions.

Examples :

(199)
Joy (High).

(200)
Despair (Deep).

(201)
Geniality (Wide).

(202)
Modesty (Narrow).

(203)
Welcome (Forward).

(204)
Distaste (Backwards).

Many variations of the simple roots can be found, and a recognisable pattern of movement emerges from the foundation of the dimensions and their expressive significance. A strong emotion or attitude of mind will result in a strong movement. If environment or conditioned training do not allow the strong movement to be made externally, concentrated inner tension of equal strength will be set up. A light thought or feeling will give rise to a light movement.

In studying the dimensions, it is important for the dancer to realise that they are only a means of clarifying direction of movement as it flows through the body, and a means whereby she can bring her natural expression into an ordered form. It is necessary for her therefore to have regular practice in sequences and studies built upon them.

THE DIMENSIONAL SCALES [1]

A harmonious series of movements can be developed into a sequence, by keeping a regular order to form a scale.

Example : High–Deep, Narrow–Wide, Backwards–Forwards.

This will be found a good basic order to establish, from which a great variety of movements can be linked fluently and harmoniously to bring in all parts of the body.

A very valuable practice for co-ordination and continuity is that of making a swinging figure of eight into each of these directions. By leading the swings with the arms, great volume in each movement is acquired.

Example :

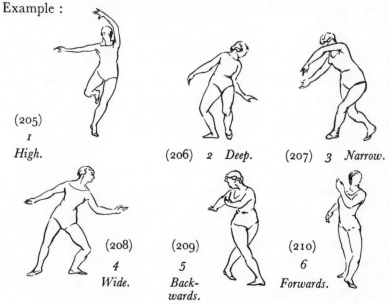

(205)

1

High.

(206) 2 Deep.

(207) 3 Narrow.

(208)

4

Wide.

(209)

5

Back-
wards.

(210)

6

Forwards.

The Dimensional Scale with an Eight Swing lead by the Left Arm.

[1] See Author's Note, page 6.

It is also possible to do the eight swings with both arms in canon. This is not intended to be a test of mathematical virtuosity, but rather to allow each arm to be related through the swinging centre of the body where co-ordination of the limbs lie.

Example :

R. Arm.	1 Narrow.	2 Wide.	3 Backwards.
L. Arm.	High.	Deep.	Narrow.

R. Arm.	4 Forwards.	5 High.	6 Deep.
L. Arm.	Wide.	Backwards.	Forwards.

The Dimensional Scale with an Eight Swing with arms in Canon.

Another kind of swing taken on the path of the Dimensional Scale gives dynamic and expressive variety and is the complementary movement to the Eight Swing.

THE INVERTED SWINGS

As the name suggests, these swings start on a rise instead of on a fall as in the ordinary swing but follow the same order on the Dimensional Scale and are continuous like the Eight Swings. They have a refreshing resilience and allow great mobility in the spine.

It is possible to start with the Eight Swings lead by the Right or the Left arm, and continue without pause into the Inverted Swings which will lead again into Eight Swings.

Diagram 8

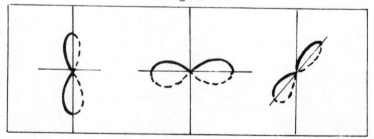

Showing the relationship between the ordinary Eight Swing and the Inverted Swing on each dimension. In diagrammatic form.

(217)	(218)	(219)
1	*2*	*3*
High	*Deep*	*Narrow*

(220)	(221)	(222)
4	*5*	*6*
Wide	*Backwards*	*Forwards*

The Inverted Swings with the Left Arm.

The expression of the Eight Swing is that of weight and ease, whilst that of the Inverted Swing is of buoyancy and action.

SUMMARY OF THE THREE DIMENSIONS [1]

First Dimension.	High–Deep.	Running in the line of gravity.
Second Dimension.	Narrow–Wide.	Running through the span of arms sideways.
Third Dimension.	Backwards–Forwards	Running through the line of advance in the legs.

Expressive content of the Dimensions :

First Dimension.	Release and Bondage.
Second Dimension.	Doubt over Trust.
Third Dimension.	Antipathy and Sympathy.

Dimensional Scales :

Movement sequences in the established order of High–Deep, Narrow–Wide, Backwards–Forwards.
The Eight Swings on the Dimensional Scale.
The Inverted Swings on the Dimensional Scale.

THE FOUR BASIC DESIGNS

In studying the Dimensions and their expressive significance, the dancer is primarily interested in finding clear-cut directions in space through which to convey articulately the content of her movement. It is possible, however, to vary the shape of the movement as it travels along its directed path in space. The tendency of a movement towards a curve or a straight line has already been referred to in the Technique section (Starting Points) where it was shown that the order in which the joints become active, determines the shape of the movement.

It is possible to classify these in terms of four basic designs. The first is a straight line which goes by the most direct path to its aim. In order to do this, the joints in arm or leg co-ordinate in action to carry the hand or foot along its straight path. In the spine, the head, chest or pelvis can be carried separately along a straight path by means of a double bend in the spine.

[1] See Author's Note, page 6.

Example :

The right leg is drawn straight up, the left leg carries the body straight down. The right hand is drawn straight up the side of the body and the left hand is thrust straight upwards. The pelvis is shifted to the left, the chest to the right, and the head juts straight forward.

The name given to all movements of this type is Droit. The expression is always direct and out-spoken, and if taken slowly, is compelling in its inevitable destination.

(223)

Jazz Number.

By the nature of the anatomical composition of the body, Droit movements have to be prepared for by a muscular adjustment and frequently necessitate a movement of another design for this preparation.

Whenever and wherever it occurs, a Droit Movement is direct and one dimensional.

The next design to be studied is a half circle curve. This is produced in the arms and legs by means of the bending of the elbow and knee joint, and in the spine by a bend in the waist or neck. The action of these bending joints brings the two ends of a limb or the trunk nearer to each other on a half circular path, and carries them away again on the same curving path.

Example :

The left knee is bringing the hips nearer to the ankle, and the right foot is moving up towards the back of the thigh. The spine and head bend over in a backwards curve, while the right hand opens out from the shoulder and the left hand has closed in to the shoulder. The name given to all opening and closing movements of this type is Ouvert. The expression is easy and economical. Taken slowly it is gracious and gentle, or if

(224)

Prayer.

with strength, it can convey veneration. A quick Ouvert can have a swinging nonchalance. In ordinary use, Ouvert movements are usually extended and aided by other designs, but in special study for dance expression they create their own style and atmosphere.

Wherever and whenever an Ouvert movement occurs, it is two dimensional and produces a half circular path.

The next design is especially connected with the rotatory joints in the body. When these joints work in sequence with the bending joints, a winding path is produced along the determined direction. In the limbs, a shoulder and hip rotation is immediately followed by a bending of the elbow or knee. In the spine and head, a rotation precedes the bend into the chosen direction.

Example :

In making the forward bend of body and head, and the raising of the forearms, the trunk has first been rotated to the right, the left shoulder rotated inwards and the right shoulder outwards. The forward leg has also been outwardly rotated before bending.

The name given to all movements of this (225) nature is Tortillé. The expression is complex *An elaborate salutation.* and personal, and according to the speed and degree of tension or relaxation contained in the movement, it can be superficially decorative or deeply emotion.

Whenever and wherever a Tortillé movement occurs, it is three dimensional and has an S-like curve.

The last design is the full circle. This is made by the rotatory joints of the body as well, but in-stead of rotating the limb or trunk round its own axis only, as in part of the tortillé movements, the limb or trunk also revolves around its centre point.

Example :

The Trunk, Head and Arms all follow the large circling movement of the body from the hips. In order to complete the full circle, the body   (226)   *Trunk Circling.*

must rotate on its own axis as well. In order to complete a full circle without a rotation, the whole body must be flung backwards in a back flip or sideways in a cartwheel, or spun round on the spot.

The name given to all movements which describe a complete circle is Rond, and the expression contained in them is that of full physical vigour. Up to a point, continued Rond movements are exhilarating, but a constant repetition of one Rond movement can induce an almost hypnotic state.

Wherever and whenever they occur, Rond movements are completely circular and two dimensional.

SUMMARY OF THE FOUR BASIC DESIGNS[1]

Droit : a direct path, one dimensional, produced by co-ordination of all joints.

Ouvert : a half circular path, two dimensional, produced by the bending joints.

Tortillé : a winding S path, three dimensional, produced by the sequence of action from rotatory to bending joints.

Rond : a circular path, two dimensional, produced by the full function of rotatory and bending joints in co-ordination.

EXPRESSION

Droit : direct and purposeful.

Ouvert : balanced and simple.

Tortillé : personal and complex.

Rond : complete participation in physical action.

PLANES OF MOVEMENT[1]

The natural movement of untrained people does not take clear-cut paths in space as do those of the dancer, but in codifying

[1] See Author's Note, page 6.

natural movement for purposes of study, the dancer is relating her special style to the normal movement habits of human beings in order to show with clarity what is unconsciously known and done by everyone. From the study of the Dimensions and the Basic Designs which are possible along the six directions of the dimensions, the dancer passes on to the study of Planes of Movement. These are the natural development from a line. Each Plane is composed of a rectangle made by combining each dimension with one other.

Diagram 9

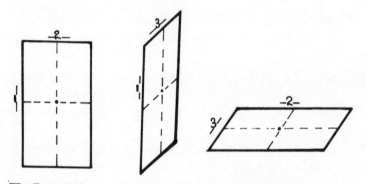

The Frontal Plane.   The Sagittal Plane.   The Horizontal Plane.
Combining Dimensions 1 and 2.   Combining Dimension 1 and 3.
Combining Dimension 1 and 3.

Anatomically certain parts of the body move more easily in one plane than another, and so the same correlation exists between the dance expression and the plane as it does in the other classifications of direction and design. The plane gives a fuller and richer source for the dancer to draw upon. In referring to dance movements which are composed only within these three planes of movement, the terms Flat, Steep, or Floating are used.

Examples :

(227)   (228)

Flat movements (movements in the frontal plane).

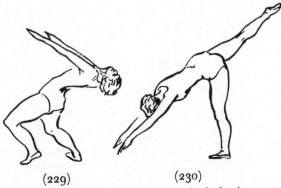

(229)   (230)

Steep movements (movements in the sagittal plane).

[1] See Author's Note, page 6.

(231)   (232)   (233)

Floating movements (movements in the horizontal plane).

The character and expression of these movements will depend, of course, on the particular bias towards one dimension or another of which the plane is composed.

Examples :
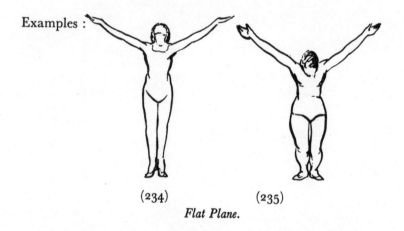

(234)   (235)

Flat Plane.

In the first example, the accent is upwards and outwards, giving a harmonious ascendancy of release and trust.

In the second, the upward lift of the arms is in contradiction to the downward line of the body. The expression of release and trust is denied by the bondage of the body, making for a dramatic pathos of unattainable aspiration.

Many variations of expression can be found within each plane. It is possible to move round the edges of the planes, across from corner to corner through the centre, or from one plane to another at the points of intersection outside the body.

Examples :

(236)
Round the Steep Plane.

(237)
Through the Flat Plane.

Many rich sequences and studies can be built on the planes and combined with steps, jumps and turns.

SUMMARY OF THE PLANES [1]

Flat Plane (the frontal plane of movement) composed of the first
    and second dimension. Contains all movements except those
    that advance or retreat.

Steep Plane (the sagittal plane of movement) composed of the
    first and third dimension. Contains all movements except
    those that narrow and widen.

Floating Plane (the horizontal plane of movement) composed of
    the second and third dimension. Contains all movements
    except those that rise and fall.

THE SPACE DIAGONALS [1]

The dancer is now ready to classify full three dimensional
movements in terms of what she has learnt in her study of
dimensions and planes, and the simplest of the regular solid
shapes to base this classification on is the Cube.

By imagining herself to be at the intersecting point of the
three dimensions, the dancer gets six clear directions, and three
clear areas of movement, but it is not until she includes a diagonal
line of movement in her classification that she can become fully
mobile and completely expressive. This necessitates starting out
from the centre of an imaginary Cube.

Starting from the centre of the body it is possible to move
outwards in eight diagonal directions along four paths.

Diagram 10

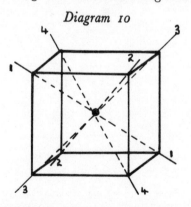

The nature of these movements is unlike those of the dimensions and planes as the axis falls outside the vertical line of gravity.
The expression of these imaginary paths in space is infinite as they
lie outside the ordinary limitations of the three dimensions. A
diagonal line of movement gives a sense of volume and portent
even when supported on a stable base.

[1] See Author's Note, page 6.

MOVEMENTS ON FOUR SPACE DIAGONALS

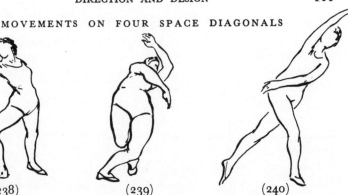

(238)	(239)	(240)
Forwards High Wide.	*Backwards Deep Narrow.*	*Forwards High Narrow.*

(241)	(242)	(243)
Backwards Deep Wide.	*Backwards High Narrow.*	*Forwards Deep Wide.*

(244)	(245)
Backwards High Wide.	*Forwards Deep Narrow.*

In order to get the feel of the spaciousness and freedom of these movements, the dancer must have a great deal of practice in moving freely and continuously from one diagonal to another.

It is possible to swing round the centre over three space diagonals and keep in continuous labile motion.

By linking different diagonals and levels, a very rich vocabulary of movements can be found which will give the dancer great breadth and confidence physically, and will allow complete expressive amplitude.

According to the rules of form and content slowly being built up in the dancer's training, each Space Diagonal will have its own particular attribute depending upon the particular combination of directions of which it is composed.

SUMMARY OF THE FOUR SPACE DIAGONALS

Eight directions lying on four diagonal lines that intersect at the centre.

Each diagonal is composed of three directions.

1. High Wide Forwards and Deep Narrow Backwards.

2. High Narrow Forwards and Deep Wide Backwards.

3. High Narrow Backwards and Deep Wide Forwards.

4. High Wide Backwards and Deep Narrow Forwards.

Continuous movements between these diagonals are Labile as their balance line is outside the vertical axis.

Expressive content follows the same tendencies as the dimensions and planes.

The foregoing main classification of directions in space from the centre of the body together with the four main designs which may be made along any of these paths, form the groundwork of all the movements that are centred in or around the body, and it is from these structural lines that a highly skilled and harmoniously composed technique springs. Two large Main Scales of Movement have been established as a useful framework with a smaller one which acts as a starting point for many more. Advanced classification goes on beyond that based on the Cube, to include the movements that are outside and around the body, but not centred within it. The two regular solids used for the classification of these finer peripheral movements, are the Dodecahedron and the Icosahedron. A separate volume deals with this advanced work which makes possible a classification of movements within a complete sphere.

THE AXIS SCALE [1]

This is the preliminary scale to the two main central scales, all of which are built upon the relationship between the corners of the three planes and the spaces between their surfaces which contain the space diagonals.

[1] See Author's Note, page 6.

Example : Select one Space diagonal and join together six movements made by starting from the corner of one of the planes. Continue by travelling alternately up and down the chosen diagonal, visiting the corner of a different plane each time until the starting point is reached again.

Example :

Diagram 11

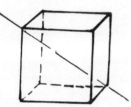

Space Diagonal to be used.

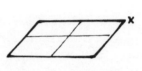

Start at corner of Floating Plane.

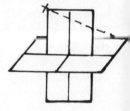

1. Move up *to top corner Flat Plane.*

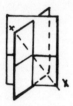

2. Move down *to corner of Steep Plane at Back.*

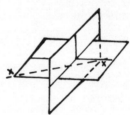

3. Move up *to corner of Floating Plane at front.*

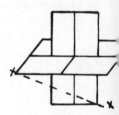

4. Move down *to bottom corner of Flat Plane.*

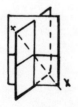

5. Move up *to corner of Steep Plane in front.*

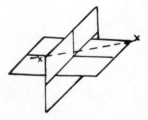

6. Move down *to original starting point on Floating Plane.*

These six movements keep a regular order in that the first movement is towards the Flat Plane, the second towards the Steep, the third towards the Floating. From here the sequence starts again with a Flat movement, a Steep movement and a Floating movement. It will be remembered that Flat, Steep and Floating movements were studied as two dimensional designs in the study of the three planes of movement. These terms are still retained in the identification of the separate movements of the main scales built on the diagonals. Each movement takes a main diagonal path but has a bias towards the plane towards which it is travelling.

Movement from an Axis Scale

(246)
Start.

(247)
Flat.

(248)
Steep.

(249)
Floating.

(250)
Flat.

(251)
Steep.

(252)
Floating.

Similar scales can be made on each of the four Space Diagonals.

By this means the movements of these Scales have a full three-dimensional sweep over space between the stable corner points of the planes. These corners serve only as guidance and in order that clarity may not be sacrificed to volume. The value of the Scales for the dancer is the feel of the generous flow out in space between the stable points. A knowledge only of the shape of the position reached at each point is valueless as these are static and only of consequence in their relation to the sweep of movement before and after.

THE A AND B SCALES

The largest continuous circuit of main movements that can be made on the space diagonals are twelve in number. These are made on the same principle as the Axis Scale but take in three diagonals, the fourth being the axis round which the circuit is formed. The two scales are complementary, each movement having a mirror of itself in the other scale.

Movements from the A Scale.

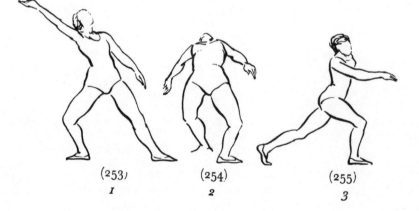

(253)   (254)   (255)

1   *2*   *3*

(256)
4

(257)
5

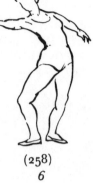

(258)
6

(259)
7

(260)
8

(261)
9

(262)
10

(263)
11

(264)
12

For purposes of reference and identification, the movements of the two main scales (A and B) are given numbers from zero, through one to twelve, to infinity. This is convenient and useful, but it must be remembered that the number refers to the kind of movement and its content and is not a constant point in space. Dancers and teachers must guard strongly against allowing the scientific basis of classification to devitalise the full rhythmic sweep of the movement in its inevitable course. It cannot be overemphasised that a theoretical knowledge of the composition of the scales is useless and even harmful, unless they have been done practically. Some dancers will approach their work first through the intellect and others through a personal experience. This is an individual thing and no rules can be laid down as to the order of approach. What is essential is that both approaches be made. One without the other will not produce a finished artist, a complete teacher or a whole person.

SUMMARY OF THE SCALES

The Axis Scale.   A complete circuit of six continuous movements around the axis of any one space diagonal.

The A Scale.   A complete circuit of 12 continuous movements made up of 4 from each of 3 space diagonals, all taken round the axis of the fourth.

The B Scale.   The complementary scale to the A scale. This contains the four movements around the axis omitted from the A Scale.

All Scales follow the order of Flat, Steep and Floating movements and travel alternately up and down the diagonals for halfway, then alternately down and up the diagonals for halfway.

All movements are referred to by numbers. 1–12 in the A Scale. B Scale is composed of 4 movements from the A Scale (8, 5, 2, 11). 4 reversed movements from the A Scale (9, 6, 3, 12), plus 4 movements that do not occur in the A Scale (right and left zero, right and left infinity).

CHAPTER V

IMPROVISATION AND COMPOSITION

IMPROVISATION is the raw material from which Composition grows. It is not within the province of this volume to discuss the therapeutic, educational or social value of creative work. It is sufficient to lay down certain guiding lines for the development of the creative potentiality of the dancer and teacher.

Improvisation as part of dance training sets out to provide a stimulus for a natural and undeliberated response. The nature and variety of these stimuli are many. They can, however, be broadly classified in relation to the senses by means of which the impact is received.

STIMULI FOR IMPROVISATION

1. Audible.

2. Visual.

3. Tactile.

4. Literary.

IMPROVISATION TO AUDIBLE STIMULI

This means anything that comes by way of the ear in the form of sound.

In the early stages of training all that should be considered is the quality of sound. For this there is an infinite variety of instruments to hand. The rattle of peas in a tin, the tearing and screwing of paper, the whistle of a train, the drone of an aeroplane, the crash of falling masonry can all provide a stimulus to move. The means for making different qualities of sound will be found in any studio or classroom, and can be added to by passing noises in the street.

It is better to avoid a regular metric repetition in any sound as this may detract from concentration upon variability of quality. Where the noise is controllable, an increase and decrease in volume can also be made to vary the impact.

When the student has become sensitive and freely responsive to the content of sounds, an ordered rhythm can be introduced. This can be done with any of the primitive noises to hand, by drum, gong, clapping and stamping or with the voice. If the voice is used at this stage, words or sentences should be avoided, and the emphasis should be on variety in volume and pace.

Next the student can be introduced to changes in pitch and focus whilst keeping all the foregoing practices going. For this it will be necessary to have an instrument where tension can be altered to requirements. A drum can be tightened or slackened, the voice can be thrown to varying distances and a string can be shortened or lengthened. By building up slowly in this way, the natural response of the student can be developed more deeply and she will be better prepared for improvisation to music. A sensitive musician should be allowed to come in with the students' improvisations at this stage, following rhythmically and dynamically and avoiding where possible a too regularly set metre. Only in the final stages of improvisation should set music be used when the student has covered the groundwork in a free way.

When using audible stimuli in this way the purpose of the sound is to convey movement directly to the body. A dancer who already has a technical vocabulary of movement may tend to draw stock movements from it in answer to any idea suggested by the sounds. This is not an immediate or spontaneous response, and the purpose of this stage of improvisation is lost. The aim here is to develop immediate sensitivity in the body to the " feel " of the changing strength, speed and flow of the sounds, and their forms or pitch. A soft noise close at hand has a different feel from a loud noise afar off although both may have the same degree of audibility. The sound of a drum being beaten has a different feel from that of a gong although both may have the same volume and speed.

IMPROVISATION TO VISUAL STIMULI

This means anything that comes by way of the eyes.

The aims in the first stages are the same as those in the use of Audible Stimuli, i.e., to obtain an immediate and un-deliberated response to the feel of what the eye conveys, rather than a movement following an idea associated with what is seen.

Colours should be used in as many contrasts as possible. Light and dark, warm and cold, strong primaries, soft secondaries, hard and soft, and gradations from one to another. Materials, papers, colour wash strokes could all be used. The dancer's response would be very much an inner feeling of mood or atmosphere with less external movement than at a later stage.

It is possible to suggest movement in space by arranging colours in such a way that some by contrast " come forward " and others " go back ". In dance training, however, the early stage of colour stimulation would take its place with the rest of spontaneous response to stimuli.

Shape and design can be shown in objects, drawings on a blackboard or traced in the air. The aim is for the dancer to get the feel of the flow and relationship of lines or curves, to sense the difference between large and small, light and heavy, static and dynamic, harmonious and discordant, in the body.

Later, she can move from one shape to another with a har-monious design, sensing the flow from large to small, light to heavy, and gradually building up a rhythmic and ordered design of movement.

There should be no musical accompaniment to visual im-provisation at this stage. When the dancer is able to feel a body rhythm in harmony with the feel of the shape and the flow of design, and can move it freely in her body and in outer space, a pianist can pick up this rhythm and come in sympathetically with an accompaniment. It would be unwise to allow music at an earlier stage. An audible stimulus would detract from the visual in these early stages.

It is important that the dancer allows the general impression to act upon her rather than specific detail of outline.

Finally, the student can be introduced to animated design seen in plants and animals. The dancer would not be attempting to look like a wave, a bird or a bear. These subjects would serve to convey only an ordered design of rhythm.

Throughout all the stages of visual stimuli, the aim is to develop immediate sensitivity in the body to the feel of changing tone, level and extension of colour and line, and the flow and speed of these in animation. An expanse of calm grey sea has a different content from a lightning flash.

TACTILE STIMULI

This means anything that comes by means of touch.

Physiologically this would include the senses of taste and smell, but this would be too esoteric a classification for improvisation stimuli. Practice in the feel of different textures and the sensitivity to them of different parts of the body would be the first stage. Choose contrasting surfaces and outlines to convey the difference between rough and smooth, sharp or rounded. Next compare heavy with light, large with small, resilient with slack.

After this, feel the varying strength, weight and speed of mechanical or natural forces. The sting of an electric shock and the undertow of a receding wave, the brushing of a cat's tail, and the clasp of a dank hand.

Finally, with a partner, try to receive a movement through touch and pass it on to someone else. This can then be built up into an ordered rhythm of movements and passed on from one to another.

As in the case of the stimuli by ear and by eye, the dancer's aim is to develop sensitivity and immediate response to the changing tensions, outlines and patterns of inanimate matter, together with the flow and speed of animate matter.

The basis of all the foregoing stimuli has been a rhythmic communication direct to the body through the senses. While taken separately for purposes of classification, it will be seen that there is an overlapping as each particular stimulus has something in common with the other two. The teacher's use of these methods in the training of the dancer is guided entirely by the needs of her student. It must be remembered that the aim throughout is to induce sensitivity and response in the body in order that the dancer may improvise freely and draw upon her own rhythmic vitality. With a wide range of stimuli, many combinations of the elements of movement will be found. In addition to free improvisation on the suggested lines, the dancer should be allowed also to lead the improvisation of others. By using her own voice, beating a drum or gong, selecting colours and shapes, her own observation and versatility will improve.

LITERARY STIMULUS

This kind of stimulus is basically different from those described. By suggesting a mood, an atmosphere or a situation, a mental image is created. This has to be translated into bodily feeling after its communication to the mind.

Many dancers will find this an easier method. In the early development of the creative potentiality of each dancer, however, the mood, atmosphere or situation should arise out of her own movement. After a good deal of free improvisation, a dancer should be able to create a mood or atmosphere in her body at will, and from this develop a movement rhythm which can be repeated and developed. It is at this point that the dancer begins to compose.

COMPOSITION IN GENERAL

The essence of Modern Dance Training is its potentiality for individual creative work based upon an understanding of fundamentals through practical experience. Every teacher and dancer should be able to compose training Studies and Dances which are more than a hyphenated set of exercises. The purpose of the Study is to impart certain principles to the dancer's bodily understanding. The purpose of the Dance is to communicate to the spectator certain feelings or thoughts. In both cases there are stages of development.

The Study is based upon a theme which arises from a technical, dynamic or a spatial design principle, and is concerned with the dancer's own understanding. Spectators are not necessary and no specific communication is made. The dancer is concerned with her own body, mood or pattern. When, however, these three things are integrated in one composition, in order to communicate, a dance is made, and needs the participation of a spectator.

The Study should never be regarded as a repetitive exercise for purposes of training one aspect only. If the theme is a Technical one, it must not be divorced from Dynamics and Design in its execution. If a Dynamic Study is composed, correct placing and clarity of line must not be neglected. A Study in Design must be felt by the dancer and executed with technical competence. In this way the composition and execution of a Study prepares the way for dance choreography.

DANCE COMPOSITION AND CHOREOGRAPHY

There can be no set rules for composition and choreography, but an outline of certain essentials may be useful.

CHOICE OF THEME

In the early stages of composition, the dancer should be primarily concerned with the expression of her own feeling and how she can convey this to the spectator. She should therefore begin with a solo dance which expresses some particular harmony or clash of mood experienced by her. It is possible that this will have emerged during her free improvisation periods, or be taken from an everyday experience or feeling. If she has difficulty in deciding upon a theme of this nature, she should choose a character or a situation from which she can extract the moods.

PROCEDURE FOR SOLO DANCE

Having broadly set a mood, character, or situation, she should move about under its influence to get the " feel " of it, until she can begin to observe what she is doing. As soon as she can observe herself while she is feeling, she is ready for the next stage. She can then either go right through to the end in this way, broadly getting the feeling of what is possible next, or start the next stage with what she has. For purposes of clarity here, we will assume that she has sketched roughly the development of mood to the end, and is able to observe herself while doing so. The next stage is a process of clarifying the technical execution. The dancer must now study the changing degrees of strength and speed, levels, direction and design of her improvisation and work out steps to form clear rhythmic phrases. This process is similar to forming words into sentences, in order to convey an idea. Throughout her training the dancer has been working on fundamental principles as they operate in her own body, and it is from these that she draws when composing.

The final stage is presentation. Having developed a mood or idea, sketched it in roughly, worked out the exact technical execution and rhythmic phrasing, the dancer will already have become aware of her relationship to the room in which she is working. She must also relate her dance clearly in floor pattern to the working space and her approach to the spectator. Relationship and approach play a big part in choreography and more will be said about them later. The solo dance is the simplest to start on as the dancer has only her own space relationship and approach to consider.

USE OF MUSIC

Music is usually an integral part of dancing, but unless it is specially composed for the purpose, it can deplete the rich potentiality of movement expression. The ideal way is for dancer and musician to compose together as they go along. In her early compositions the dancer very often relies a great deal upon set music. Circumstances often make it necessary for her to work to gramophone records. These impose limitations upon her while giving her a certain amount of guidance. In using pre-selected set music the dancer can be inventive and interpretive, but to be truly creative she needs to be able to compose from her own imaginative and kinaesthetic sense. This can be done in several ways.

1. By dancing without music.

2. By dancing to percussion, words or any accompaniment which has arisen out of the dance idea and is arranged by the dancer.

3. By composing the dance in the main, searching for set music which supplies the right atmosphere, and adjusting the dance where necessary.

4. Where possible, by working with a musician who can follow her movements and compose for them.

The dancer must always remember that dancing is not only musical interpretation. She should use music intelligently and with respect. She should not keep slavishly to a time beat, ignoring the rhythm and structure of the whole. She should never regard music as her servant, nor her master, but always as her partner.

In the processes of improvisation to varying stimuli, the dancer will finally use set music to which to improvise. A wide choice of types of music and composers should enable the dancer to begin and continue a broad study of music whether or not she is able to play an instrument. As she grows in knowledge and experience of her own art, the dancer will find many familiar principles in other art forms and should be alive to the pattern common to all arts. In this way she will learn to understand and respect other art forms, and in using music for her dance compositions will avoid the mistake of treating it merely as a time-keeper.

PROCEDURE FOR DANCE FOR TWO OR THREE

In the main, dance choreography for two or three dancers develops by the same stages as a Solo Composition, but the factor of relationships becomes more important. The dancer is no longer solely occupied in the early stages with her own emotional expression but with her relationship to her partner or partners. She must feel and observe from the start, and every stage of development must be regarded in relation to her partners. It is possible for dancers to get the broad " feel " of the whole thing together, and then to clarify technically each for herself, coming together again to test and observe the pattern made between them. Dancers must find the most satisfactory method for themselves, but should aim at a mutual contribution.

PROCEDURE FOR GROUP DANCE

In order to compose a satisfactory Group Dance by the same stages as the above methods, a high degree of group sensitivity is necessary. The importance of a dance of this nature is less on individual movement than on the emotional content of the mass. Technique and performance of steps will be dominated by the size and formation of the group. Levels, directions and floor patterns, however, can be made great use of. Relationships within the group, splitting and rejoining, can have many variations.

After the roughing-in has been done to get the " feel " of the development, a few people at a time should stand out to observe the general shape and trend. Finally, every individual should know her own spot or area of operation in relation to the group, the working area and the spectator.

CHOREOGRAPHY FOR OTHERS

The most profitable experience for the dancer is to compose solo dances for herself, and also to work with others in composing dances for twos, threes or a group. This will enable her to get personal experience, to develop awareness of other people and sensitivity to their needs and demands, and the " feel " of different relationships and formations. When she is confronted with a group of people with whom she has to create a dance, the process will be the sum total of her experiences and observations of the above methods.

Broadly, the dancer must familiarise herself with the following choreographic points :

1. Expression in bodily design.
2. Body attitude and Floor Pattern.
3. Relationships.

EXPRESSION IN BODILY DESIGN

This has been dealt with in general in the section on Direction and Design. Anatomically the body is shaped according to function, but as expression of emotion, and intention of will, are conveyed by means of the body, the patterns of movement follow the same design.

Physically, the body is divided into Head, Arms, Legs and Trunk, each part having a major function to fulfill.

The Head serves to orientate the whole body and exercise a control and guidance upon it. Arms are used for protection or attack as they have maximum range of movement, and with the special power of the hand, can grasp, reject and explore. The Legs have a similar function but are restricted in range. Their main function is to support and mobilise the body, and in this way extend the possibilities of the sphere of action of the hands and arms. The Feet, like the Hands, can grasp, reject and explore, and in certain cases the functions of Arms and Legs can be interchangeable. The Trunk is the vital centre wherein lies the creation and preservation of life, and the co-ordination of all the parts to the whole.

Expressions of emotion or thought will arise from the physical area related to the nature of the expression.

Broadly, an action arising in or lead by the Head will be objective. Actions of hands and feet in their simplest form are practical. But if the hand or foot follows a movement which has arisen in another part of the arm or leg, the expression will be less simple and practical according to the part of the arm or leg in which the movement originated. Actions originated in the Trunk are largely subjective, but again are tempered with the expression of the particular part of the Trunk from which they arise.

For the choreographer a basically simple pattern emerges from this. The body expression can be divided roughly into Intellectual, Emotional and Aesthetic. The emotions lie nearest to the centre, and the intellect lies nearer to the surface, whilst in between these is a strata of consciousness of feeling which stems from both thought and feeling, In expressive movement of the body, therefore, actions arising nearer to the body centre are the most deeply emotional.   In the limbs and head, action arising in the upper arm, thigh and back of the neck, carries more feeling than that nearer to the extremities or face.   Trunk movements that start in the upper part of the chest are more aesthetic than those that originate nearer the centre of gravity, while movement that is a result of a conscious thought process will be lead by the face or the hands.   For the choreographer, subtleties of expression can be conveyed by careful exploration into the varying degrees of conscious awareness and reflex physical reaction that are contained in each thought or feeling, and for which there will be the corresponding area of activity in the body.   Between feeling at the centre and thought at the extremities there are many possible combinations of both.

BODY ATTITUDE

The nature of the four fundamental designs and their expressive significance has already been discussed.   These are of use to the choreographer in establishing the nature of the dancer's approach to a person or situation.

The inner state of mind or feeling shows itself in small movements of body, face, hands and feet, and although these may not be large enough to classify as main movements, yet their pattern of behaviour is the same.   A clear-cut approach mentally will be conveyed in a direct focusing of attention with an undeviating line of posture.   This can be directed outwards or inwards, but in either case the feeling will be that of a line of concentration.

A softer approach brings about a rounding of outline and the postural attitude is less directly stated and focused.   Where there is an objective mental approach tempered with personal feeling, the general pattern of body attitude will be gently curving.

A more vigorously felt attitude of mental and physical well-being expresses itself in a fully rounded curve, where every pattern seems to be nearing a full circle.

Finally, an acutely self-conscious attitude brings about a twisting curve that curls around itself and is deeply focused upon itself.   These four basic patterns of external movement, reflex actions, attitudes of mind and shades of expression, are carried

MD—9

out also in the path taken by the dancer in her approach across the floor.

FLOOR PATTERN

A straight path has purpose and decision, whilst a curved path is less aggressive. It can be friendly, a little self-effacing, in fact a harmonious link between two things or people.

The twisted path shows emotional activity, with disturbances of feeling as the sweeping changes of direction occur. Changes of direction made by broken straight lines instead of changing curves, convey lack of decision, mental confusion and inner restlessness. The completely circular path indicates enjoyment for its own sake or an external compulsion to continue indefinitely.

In using these basic indications of design in the body, in attitude, posture and floor track, the choreographer must find a combination of these and the basic dynamics which contains what he wishes to say. For clarity, he can divide each part of the body into an area of Mental Awareness and Physical Response. From this fundamental concept he can build a language of thought and feeling through design and dynamics.

RELATIONSHIPS

Throughout the whole of her training the dancer has had to bring herself into alignment. First of all, within her own body she has been training towards good posture, co-ordination of all parts of the body to the whole, balance and economy of effort. Next she has compared, blended, contrasted and balanced emotional qualities, and studied the significance of pattern and design. Finally she has developed her sensitivity and response to external things, conditions and people. As a composer and choreographer, she must bring all these things into relationship, not only within the individual dancer, but between dancer and dancer, group and group, dancer and spectator, group and spectator.

This process can be classified as follows :

BASIC FORMATIONS
FOR TWO DANCERS

(265)
Meeting.

1. Full facing.

This implies a basic mutual response. The degree and nature of the response will vary with body design, attitude and floor pattern, but the significance of the formation remains.

Accompanying.

2. Side by side.

This implies a common purpose or situation. The nature of the purpose or situation will vary with changes in body design, attitude and floor pattern, but the significance of the formation remains.

Passing.

3. Side by side (reversed).

This implies a fleeting contact which can be prolonged by variations in body design, attitude and floor pattern, but must ultimately be lost.

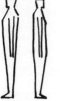

(268)
Relinquishing.

4. Back to back.

This implies separation of purpose or situation. This can be bridged by variations in body design, attitude and floor pattern, but the basic significance remains.

From these basic formations combinations can be made as under :

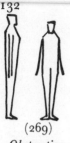

(269)

Obstructing.

5.

This implies conflict of purpose or situation. This can be partially resolved by variations in body design, attitude and floor pattern, but the basic significance remains.

(270)

Upholding.

6.

This implies a converging of purpose or situation. This can be developed by variation in body design, attitude and floor pattern, but the basic significance of the formation remains.

(271)

Leading and following.

7.

This implies the unknown and creates a weaker and a stronger. Which is the weaker and which the stronger is determined by variations of body design, attitude and floor pattern, but the unknown remains.

The above examples of relationships implicit in formations are seen to be the basis of collective formations, and the individuals' relationship within them.

BASIC COLLECTIVE FORMATIONS

1. The Rank.

This implies collective display, but lack of individual personality. This can be achieved by a contrast of body design or attitude.

(272)

2. The File.

This implies collective purposeful action but an individual hierarchy.

(273)

3. The Circle.

This implies a common acceptance with individual equality and mutual response.

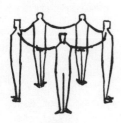

(274)

(*a*) *Facing in.*

This implies a mutual concealment or defence with individual equality.

(275)

(*b*) *Facing out.*

The above basic formations for two and any number more than two form the root from which all the groups stem.

GROUPS

A collection of people is not necessarily a group, and an individual can be in a group but not of it. Broadly, a group is formed by a common purpose or a common situation. Within a loose group there can be smaller groups and individuals, each with their own formations and relations, but these must also bear relationship to the whole to remain part of the group.

The final use of grouping is the culmination of the choreographers art. In the brief references given here, the raw material will be found. The result can only be in the hands of the individual who wants to create from it.

The final relationship to be considered by the choreographer is that of dancers to the stage and to the audience. Many forms of production in which audience participation is possible and even essential make interesting material for experiment, but following the general trend of this book, only the basic principles of use of the " picture stage " will be given.

In presenting a solo dance or an epic ballet on a modern stage, the dancer still draws from principles of spatial design and the significance of basic formations already given. These will yield certain generalities of stage placing, exits and entrances.

STAGE PLACING

Figures occupying areas nearer the centre of the stage are more naturally dominant than those nearer the sides, backcloth or corners.

Downstage figures are stronger than upstage figures. For dramatic purposes, however, these rules can be inverted by creating a special relationship between two dancers, or two groups, whereby the dominance of one over the other is gained by a change of level, or the use of the principle of basic formations. In this case individual or group stage placing becomes secondary to the setting of the picture as a whole, in which the eye and the interest can be led by means of continuity of pattern.

The relationship of the dancer or group of dancers to the audience follows the same principle as those of basic formations. When the dancer faces her audience she is open to them and coming to meet them. In turning her back upon them she is asking them to follow or support her. When she turns to right or left, the audience is left outside and the dancer becomes impersonal.

EXITS AND ENTRANCES

When a dancer comes on to the stage the situation of her entrance will follow the same rule as Stage Placing, but her impact on the audience will be affected also by the pattern of her floor track. These have already been mentioned under the heading of Floor Pattern, and must now be taken in conjunction with the situation of the entrance.

A straight track from upstage to downstage is the most direct and presents almost an attack upon the audience.

A straight track from side to side whilst the dancer faces her audience makes a full display for the audience without attack.

A straight track from side to side which leads the dancer straight on and off, leaves the audience outside as an observer rather than a participant.

A curved track follows the same principle as the straight in its relation to its exit and entrance but, in addition, places the audience within the curve of action or outside it. A track curving from downstage to upstage leaves the audience outside. That curving from upstage to downstage includes them.

All the above generalities are intended only as simple guiding lines to the dancer, teacher and choreographer in her personal exploration and practice.

No artist can be made from a book, but it is hoped that this volume may help to clarify a method and assist all those who love dancing, and who are prepared to serve an art with study, tenacity and labour.

CHAPTER VI

LOOKING BACKWARDS AND FORWARDS

Since the publication of this volume in 1958, Modern Dance in England has continued to develop considerably both in education and in the theatre. In the physical education departments of schools, colleges and universities there has been a trend towards greater clarification and form as the natural result of the freer methods of the past two decades. This has taken broadly three forms.

A recognition of the disciplinary values of a knowledge of Laban's theory of Space Harmony is more general, and in some cases a near academic approach to these laws is showing itself. The original idea of analysis of movement for training was very broadly based on the Time, Weight, Space, Flow concept and the logical extension into the Efforts and the Dimensions served as a springboard for further activity. These fundamental principles have to a large extent become digested and established in areas outside the dance lesson, and in the physical educational field, modern dance and modern educational gymnastics are constantly being reviewed in the search for some further development which will provide a satisfactory condition of articulate individual expression and control.

While there is no lack of interest and appreciation of the value of experiment, improvisation and individual freedom, the general swing is once again towards what is called technique. The student, child and teacher is being asked to relate thinking to spontaneity. There is a much greater area of knowledge about movement and dance than ever before, and in some cases the training college student is near erudite in her ability to write, invent and analyse in terms of movement. The child and the teacher also show a greater ability to be objective in their approach to what has always been considered a subjective activity. Between the freedom of doing and the discipline of thinking, the need for technique seems to have grown.

In a world of technology, perhaps the word technique is assuming a very specific shape. In the dance world, technique has loosely been understood as the clear demonstration of the thing to be done. Since this has been regarded as an aim in itself, its use in physical education has caused divided reactions. It is a fact however, that technique has become more stylised in general in that recognisable repetitions of movements and dance steps are emerging more consistently, and the adoption of set patterns of movements from a variety of systems is seen more often. The athleticism of the American genre with its accent on youth and vigorous self assertion has moved in strongly beside the earlier psychological and emotional group activities of the European school. This mixture of astringent action and mass communication lends itself to very vigorous expression at any level. This is seen in the rise of interest in Jazz Ballet, Dance Drama, Pop and Folk, and anything which is vigorously meaningful to the participants through the repetition of a strong beat and freedom to create something of one's own within that beat. Wedded to a specialised technique of training this can produce telling results, but at the other end of the scale can become a self induced euphoria. In general in the physical education world, a much greater freedom to experiment within a clearly given context is seen in gymnastics and dance, but in the dance field only, there are evidences of a variety of styles becoming perpetuated as methods to be embraced or rejected according to what they have to offer the individual.

In addition to the advances in theoretical knowledge and the practice of techniques, an interest in notation is steadily growing Many rival systems have put forward claims and brought much evidence in support of the superiority of their own method. The real significance would seem to be more in the common denominator of all systems, than in the prior merits of one method over another. This common factor must surely be that an exactitude of action must be obtained before a clear description of that action can be recorded. Since movement is a highly complex phenomenon, an accurate record would seem to necessitate an equally complex form of recording. This complexity has indeed been the criticism in general that has been levelled at established forms of notation, and competition between systems often hinges around the claim to greater simplicity. And yet simplicity seems to be the one element that has suffered most in the forward steps taken in the last decade.

The advances in knowledge, technical ability and analytical power seem to have resulted on the one hand in a greater complexity of inventiveness, and on the other in a determination to reject all rules, habits and conventions of past eras. In this way, a constant build-up-break-down mechanism is at work, attempting to create a new structure by analysing the old and re-arranging it as new. The proceedures in present day theatre, music, sculpture and painting echo this tendency. One aspect of form or feeling is isolated out and an immense variety of structures is built up on this partial basis. This for a time gives an impression of simplicity, but in its development, becomes a highly complicated process of organising re-arrangements of the isolated aspect rather than an organic evolution of the whole.

This, in effect, is the situation of modern dance in physical education at the present time. Since its simple beginnings in England, some three decades ago, it has undergone considerable changes, some of which have been summarised above, and the end product is now much more sophisticated than it was in the initial stages. The physical education teacher now has many more demands made upon her in the field of art, and often finds her work leading her into literature, sculpture, painting, music and drama. Projects undertaken through the co-operation and co-ordination of the revelant departments in school or college, have produced interesting work, but the role of the gym mistress as artist is surely one to be given serious thought.

Efforts have been made in the educational system, to provide for the educational student who showed a special propensity for dance, and for some years a collaboration between courses in physical education and the arts has been established. At the present time, dance specialists are being trained to work in education either on European or American lines. This is a great advance upon the time when dancing in schools was a poor substitute for games on a wet afternoon, but it brings into light several points of interest.

If the dance specialist is trained for work in education, the question arises as to the difference between such a teacher and one trained for dance in the theatre. The obvious answer is in the end product. The teacher in education sets out to achieve certain personal improvements and developments in the child or student through the medium of dance. The professional teacher sets out to employ to the full the potential talent of the student in preparation for a professional career, where a high level of performance has to be maintained daily before an audience. In both cases the student sets out to dance, this being the activity to be taught by the teacher.

The word dance will mean different things to different people, but all will agree that it is concerned with moving in a pattern of rhythmic order which is connected with that other part of the self that is not purely physical. The natural outburst of joy in movement has been experienced by everyone at some time or another, and it is this condition, expressed in rhythmic order, that everyone recognises as dance. The problem in training is an obvious one; to extend the range of potential to its fullest whilst maintaining natural expression. These two aspects of training are loosely called, technique and expression, and as such, are more often than not separated. It is not surprising therefore that it is possible to establish two seperate attitudes to training in the same activity.

The teacher of educational dance is faced with the problem of technique. Dare she impose it at the expense of personal development and confidence? If so at what stage? And what sorts of techniques are right and suitable to her particular children or students. Whose methods can be entrusted to produce the best results? Does technique have to be imposed externally or should it automatically develop at some stage of the personal development?

These and a host of other questions have arisen for discussion and decision, and trends have been set according to trial and error methods of observation and experience.

The teacher of professional dance has similar problems in her work. She must keep up with ever increasing technical demands to meet the requirements of modern choreographers, but she must also enable her student to grow in expression and feeling as the competent machine of her body is trained. By what magic can she release or induce feeling, or will it automatically grow with the rigorous practice of daily technical routines? By running parallel classes in freer or rhythmic activities, by introducing acting techniques, by exposing the dancer to the more abandoned and uninhibited forms of pop music and dance, and by any other means available for broadening the limits of conventional dance training, the teacher seeks to open the vials of the dancer's feeling and expression.

Simplicity and ease of clearly articulated expression through a minimum of effort cannot be seen to grow under either of the foregoing conditions, and the teacher in education shares the same problem with the teacher in professional theatre. How to ensure the unified development of the personality with a growing ability in skill.

In my remarks at the end of the first edition of this volume, i said that I believed the work of Sigurd Leeder achieved the education of the person whilst training the dancer. I still believe this and am reminded of a remark of his concerning his own development. After many years of experimenting and work, he found that his technique could not ever be better than his spiritual vision. He determined from that time never to seperate the two, and that he must always be faithful to the laws of dance.

During the years since these words were written, I have had opportunities of seeing the separation of these two aspects getting wider and wider. The challenge to the teacher of dance to unite training and education, to develop technique and feeling, is a real one, and the most usual method employed, is to rely upon the method employed. What is less likely to occur in the face of this challenge to unite what has been partitioned, is for the teacher to look into the condition of the person in the student, whilst employing the chosen method.

The method of teaching or training is a useful tool to be employed by the student under guidance from the teacher, in order to produce a special result. For example, the method outlined in this book is the result of the thinking of three men, each of whom was working towards a personal vision. The importance of such a method is that it be realised as a tool only. The use made of this method does not automatically ensure satisfactory results in terms of education and training. There are many other points to be considered.

In my thirty years of teaching I have encountered and studied most methods of dance training, and have worked in education and theatre. My concern has always been the unity of the person with the dance. I have found this to be quite independent of the specific method of training employed. I have found also that teachers of every method and in any category are aware of something that seems to escape them and that sends them from one trend to another to find it.

As stated earlier, Modern Dance has developed considerably in many ways, and is now really on the map by comparison. Specialist teachers are being trained at the Art of Movement Studio and at the School of Dance and Drama at Dartington. This provides a tributary from the European and the American method. In London, the establishment of the Contemporary Dance Centre, based upon the concepts of Martha Graham, promises a professional company very soon. The establishment of a dance lectureship at a British University housed in a studio planned for practical use, indicates a change of attitude. These are encouraging signs, and opportunities to earn a living as a dance specialist are increasing. Men have entered the educational field much more fully than ever before, either through physical education or drama, and the epidemic of interest and excitement caused by West Side Story has done much to reconcile the male ego to the possibility of masculinity being expressed through dancing. Athletes have undergone ballet training and ballet dancers have become all-in wrestlers, and the general climate is more favourable than ever before for a resurgence of dance. To the teachers who have seen methods come and go, or to those who have retained the practices established for years, the problem of developing the full potential of the student for his own good or in order to get a job, remains the crux of the matter. And how can this be assured?

The daily class for the professional is a *sine qua non* in the process of training where assiduous practise of chosen exercises is maintained. The athlete and the gymnast similarly set themselves a training programme which entails specific repetition.

The teacher of educational dance employs repetitions of themes as a basis for building a vocabulary of movements which may become familiar in use and lead to further inventions. Whatever the end in view, the process concerns itself specifically with the carrying out of an exercise a required number of times, whether that exercise is a physical, a mental or an emotional activity.

The well established training method of the classical ballet has been accused of rigidity and regimentation, but as a tool, has served dancers of quality and feeling very well for many years. Where sensitivity, musicality, depth of feeling, poetic or dramatic ability, has been present in the dancer, it has never been impaired by the rigorous daily workout that she has engaged in all her working life, but whether this method of training has developed, encouraged or released these qualities is open to question.

As a reaction against the so-called rigidity of the classical training method, the modern school rejected all external disciplines in order to release new ideas and feelings. After the great burgeoning and richness of expressive outpouring, some sort of shaping was inevitable. Today the professional modern schools are as disciplined as any classical school, and in many ways, are as regimented in expression as the styles they were rebelling against. Indeed as the classical schools get more modern, so the moderns become more and more classical. And so the swing goes on.

Even in the educational dance world, a recognisable style is apparent. Practices, attitudes of mind and verbal expression are becoming stereotyped, so that even in so called free work, there is a repetitive conformity in what one can expect to see. And what does one expect to see in dance? What does one expect to see in education, in the theatre, in people? What does one hope to see? Is it something new? I do not believe so.

The fact of the sun's rising and setting brings a new day into being, but there is nothing new in the constancy of the rhythm of the sun. Man's thoughts and feelings about his environment will bring new ideas, actions and vision but there is nothing new in the relationship of man to his environment. I think perhaps it is the search for something lasting rather than something new that promotes our modern trends.

The immediate and transient appeal is seen in our pop culture, and as such, has its own validity. After a time however, standards begin to be formed and a measure of critical assessment is brought to bear even upon these immediate forms of communication, in the light of experience and knowledge. There emerges a constant from which the immediate must not depart. Our teenage Juke Box Juries demonstrate this ably. In the world of dance, I believe this constancy is the quality that teachers and students are looking for. It can be given a lot of names and appear in many guises. The real thing is rarely mistaken. I believe that brass can be mistaken for gold, but I am sure that gold can never masquerade as brass.

A real experience is the only true learning in art, and for a long time in education and the theatre, these true experiences have been sought through many channels. Free dance, improvisation, experimenting, happenings, eccentricities, drugs, licence have all produced what has been claimed to be valid experiences, and the small miracle has continued to happen. But the transience remains and the search for a constant continues.

Since writing this book in 1958 I have become convinced that the only lasting good lies within each individual, and that until the teacher has a means for helping the student to tap this source herself, she is fighting a losing battle. No matter what method or system is employed, the final requirement is that the student be shown how to use that system to advance his own growth. The choice of system may be determined by many things and is not really the crucial point. I believe that no system can do more than the student is able to exploit within herself and I think now is the time for teachers to understand this. The following chapters deal with the results of this belief.

CHAPTER VII

DANCE DRAMA

Today is a time of experiment, a carousel of opportunity and potential. Discoveries, personalties, individualism, groups, new forms, old revivals, jargon, experiences, new words, new rules, no rules . . . anything goes as long as it can be deemed new. This is reflected in the theatre and in education, and in the worlds of dance and drama, these two fields of activity continue to affect, run parallel with or merge into one another. The term Dance Drama has become more established in education than in the theatre although works of such kind have been known in various forms since the beginning of dramatic expression.

It is to be expected that at such a time of transition and growth, old and new will meet, overlap, come into harmony and conflict, confusion and clarity, and that the new will often be seen to be the old in a new context. The establishment of the term Dance Drama has occurred as a result of many circumstances making up the general climate. In the outline contained in the previous chapter, reference was made to the accusation of rigidity and regimentation in dance and the resulting breakaway into experimental freedom. In rejecting the forms and practices prevalent at the time, the attention was naturally turned towards the sources of dance, and movement became seperated out as a study in its own right. A new Movement empire was being built which concerned itself with every aspect of human activity and thought. Movement for its own sake, movement as a means for personal expression and development, movement as an educational and socialising force, movement as a basis for specific training, spread from the physical education department to the drama department and from the educational world to the theatre. Movement became an idea. Dance and Mime had once had clear boundaries. Physical exercises and Gymnastics were clearly defined. But movement as an idea was something common to all these things and yet stood by itself with its own rules.

Today some form of movement training is part of the curriculum of an actor, a singer, a dancer or a sportsman outside the special techniques of his specific trade. In education, movement has a place as a training in itself, whether it be contained in Educational Gymnastics, Modern Dance, Creative Drama, Dance Drama or any of the many contexts in which it finds itself. Movement has found its way into the new visual arts through mobiles, light patterns, mechanical rhythms, foam sculpture and anything which concerns itself with a return to source.

The work of the Art of Movement Studio firmly established the validity of movement as a training and gave the lead to teachers and students in regarding this as a platform from which one could take off into one's chosen direction. It is natural that the majority should fail to see in this, a way to aquire skills of a highly stylised nature such as Classical Ballet, Olympic Gymnastics, Classical Mime. The general trend therefore was more towards a functional or expressive development in the form of either educational gymnastics or educational modern dance, at a personal level of achievment. It was found that a form of dramatic expression through movement aided by the rhythm of music, provided a satisfying means for individual expression at a non specific level. This use of music coupled with dramatic expression came to be called Dance Drama, and the name has remained. The use of music, movement, sound and speech, has been known since the beginning of drama as we know it, and there have been Masques, Dance Plays, Mime Dramas and every combination of the fundamental expressions of movement and voice. At this particular time of writing, Dance Drama has found a firm place in the educational world and has appeared in one form or another in the theatre. It has been found particularly useful with boys and men, teenagers and youth groups, and in fact, in any situation where there is no level of specific skill or training, or where a preconception has prejudiced attitudes towards pure dance or drama.

The widespread use of Dance Drama demonstrates its appeal to both participants and spectators, and this would argue that it is rooted in something vital. I think that this is so, but in my experience, there is a challenge in this very fact. At face value it would appear to be a very good thing to engage in a group activity which encouraged individual expression, free from over-direction or regimentation. The socialising force of this is obvious and the end product is likely to be more telling than detailed group direction, but a special process has to be found to meet the many problems revealed by this kind of work. By its own nature, flexibility and freedom are essential to allow for individual ability or lack of it, and for the employment of improvisation and experiment. Unless these are carefully controlled, neither the participant nor the spectator comes to any satisfactory conclusion of thought, action or experience, and, what might have been a vital and worthwhile project becomes a class exercise in wasteful and illiterate messing about. The popularity and practice of improvisation, experiment and the freer forms of drama is a measure of its power and the kind of work it produces has come to be recognised and widely accepted. I suspect that this very fact conceals some of its pitfalls and dangers. By what process can one be sure of striking the balance between sloppiness and rigidity, between chaotic freedom and petrified order? How can the individual and the group be united creatively without personal loss of identity or group anarchy? How can a variety of skills, styles, training or experience be brought to a literate form capable of some sort of communication, to any general audience?

These and many other questions have been occupying my attention for some time, and in the report that follows, I should like to set down some of my findings.

I had come to the conclusion that the many trends and developments in the educational and theatrical world of dance revealed a common search for something that would work under any conditions. In my work with amateurs and professionals in dance, gymnastics, acting and singing, I was concerned with employing nondescript groups of people with widely different levels of ability and training, in a variety of theatrical projects. Like other teachers faced with a similar problem, I had to find a vehicle which would be independent of method or training and yet would be articulate and sufficiently disciplined to result in a finished piece of work. I was not happy with the plethora of work being done under the name of improvisation and experiment, which was all too often presented with apologies, justifications or explanations for its existence and yet was exposed for public viewing. Whilst I recognise group improvisation as essential for creative work, I found that there seemed to be lacking a single guiding principle at the core of it. At this time, I came into contact with a musician whose chief concern was opera, and who had been meeting similar problems in the theatre. For four years we worked together on courses, productions and training, and in the summer of 1966, Gerald Wragg and I were invited to the University of Cape Town to produce a Dance Drama. This was to be given a public run at the Little Theatre in Cape Town after our departure This challenge and the means we adopted for meeting it, has confirmed my belief in the need for teachers and producers to look again and again, not at the method but at the means employed by the actors in their reactions to the learning or rehearsing situation. In setting down our experiences in this production, I hope that teachers and producers similarly challenged may be stimulated to further thought.

We knew that we were to produce a work of sufficient length and general interest, to play for an unspecified time to the public. We also knew that the work required was to employ an unknown number of students to move, dance, sing and speak. We knew the size of the stage—which was very small—and we knew that the preponderence of students would be women with whom we should probably have one month to rehearse whenever their academic committments freed them. We also knew that we were expected to do something " very creative ". We had therefore to see our aim very clearly and to plan meticulously for its fulfillment.

Our hope was to provide a living experience for the actors and the audience and to organise the project in such a way that it could be conceived as an organic whole which would continue to evolve during work sessions and rehearsals. This conception brought its own problems and its own opportunities. Unlike a scripted play, the Dance Drama has no life until it is brought into action through the bodies and personalities of the actors or students taking part. Unlike the specifically trained dancer who has already a vocabulary of highly stylised movements . . .(and these in fact may act as an impediment to free moving) . . . the player in a Dance Drama has to find, out of his own experience, a satisfying movement which will be meaningful to him. In order for this to be equally meaningful to an audience, there must be some outline or context which can contain the individual creations in some related progressive order.

In the planning of the work to be produced, we found it necessary to establish a theme which could be varied in an infinity of ways, and one that could develop to some acceptable conclusion. After a great deal of selection and rejection, we found that, under such circumstances, we had to start from nothing. Here then was our theme, The Creation. We were in good company. Every artist has to do this once in a lifetime. After further thinking, talking and doing, we beat out a tenuous middle section as a development. Man was to be seen engaging in his many activities in search of his goal. The resolution we found impossible to preconceive until we had the work in front of us in some concrete form.

When we arrived in Cape Town, we had a partially composed score by Gerald Wragg for part one . . . The Creation . . . a tape of musical excerpts for part two . . . and some poetry on the side for part three if it became feasible. We had an overall idea of the shape as being from the past, throught the present by means of a linking figure or pair of figures, which would end in a resolution towards the future. The first two days were spent in exploring facilities, meeting colleagues from the departments of Music and Drama, and discussing known and unsuspected hazards. Two more days were spent meeting students and holding practical sessions in groups in order to establish a personal contact and a terminology. During these practical sessions, Gerald Wragg played for the class work. Since he was a composer and musical director, his improvisations exposed the student to the climate of music we expected to be using whilst I established through action, the sort of approach I should be employing in rehearsals. Copies of the theme and general outline were handed out and a general talk given. On the fifth day, a cast of over sixty students was grouped into self-functioning units and arrangements made for a day by day rehearsal schedule to be announced according to student and staff committments. Even as early as this, each student was entirely concerned with her own feelings or ideas about what part she wanted to play in the beginning, and the formation of the group units was based entirely upon such idea as the student could get at this stage. On the seventh day, each group had an outline of action of some sort, and by the evening of that day, we achieved a run-through of music and action of Acts 1 and 2. We were now committed and we had four clear weeks ahead of us before the opening night. It is what happened during those four weeks that seems of importance to me.

The group as a whole, comprising roughly 50 girls and 10 men, had no outstanding style or talent, but seemed to be imbued with a desire and willingness to open to any new idea or experience. They had behind them the usual training in voice, mime and movement, with a smattering of ballet training here and there. They were however completely inexperienced in what they chose to call Creative Dance Drama. As the classes and rehearsals proceeded in what was little more than the atmosphere and mood of the work, individuals began to come alive as characters. Since there was no overall regimentation of any kind yet, a sense of failure to measure up to the required standard or task, was reduced to a minimum, and each day produced a concrete result of some sort. During this time, the students began to find a self critical faculty that operated much more strongly than any outside assessment, and decisions were made to change a character or a move in order to achieve a more satisfactory personal literacy.

At the end of each day's work, the evolving individual details had to be orientated to the emerging whole. This could mean anything from rewriting a scene, composing suitable music, taping and editing existing material, making room for suitable dialogue, to scrapping the whole of a preconceived idea that had appeared to be workable in our own minds. Whilst this was done, the players only became aware of an individual progression from day to day, which slowly came to be identified with other players and ultimately with the whole work. This two-way process of stimulation between producers and players eliminated a considerable amount of waste, trial and error, because there was an overall discipline of a clearly defined outline. The apparent ease with which the work progressed arose from a growing confidence and identification in each student with the work as a whole. Spontaneity and serious thought joined hands in partnership and students became able to imagine more possibilities for themselves, and, what was more interesting, to know whether they were, or not, achieving the expression in action of what they had so imagined. It was at this point of growing awareness of themselves in the act of creating actions and ideas that a student declared herself to be unable to bring about an action that she could clearly imagine herself doing. Her own words were . . . " I can't connect my head with my feet " Another student who was now playing one of the four major roles also expressed dissatisfaction with what he was actually doing compared to what he felt he was doing. A third student found that the exercises he had been practising for relaxation, given to him in an attempt to help his general condition on stage, enabled him to reach a stage of relaxation whilst practising them, but were quite ineffective in the act of employing his imagination creatively. These three students then began to work individually with Gerald Wragg upon the problem of exploitation of talent. From this point the whole work began to hinge around this central point of performance and in a very short time, many students were working individually upon this principle. By now the work had taken quite clear shape, and details were needing attention. Two of the Drama Staff had been attending rehearsals and were beginning to evolve costumes, lighting and stage managing, and taking over responsibility for recording, editing and sound effects. The tightening up process was now imminent as we were approaching the last week which had been reserved for technical and dress rehearsals. The organising now took precedence over the organic from our point of view, but it was evident now that the students had grown so much in confidence and ease that the heart of the matter could be left in their hands. The work continued to grow from within while absolute discipline was imposed from without. We saw two performances before leaving Cape Town and we knew that the ensuing run was safe in their hands.

Once again, my experience had revealed to me the core of the problem. The process employed in the creating of a Dance

Drama makes great demands upon the director. He must know every aspect of theatrical possibilities, he must have a very clear image of what he is setting out to do, and he must have the means at his disposal for " getting something out of " his students. Each teacher or producer has his own means, but it is generally agreed that imagination stems from the subconscious. If this is to be more than a moment of inspiration or a flash of insight, some means has to be found for invoking the image, the thought or the idea, and for the further means of formulating it in terms of the artistic medium.

Most of us have our own means for " getting going " and most of us have experienced the higher level of vitality following upon stimulation. These moments are very often transitory or dependent upon continued or renewed external stimulus, and can sometimes appear to come out of the blue. The happy accident, the happening, improvisation, being on form, can all appear to be fortuitous situations or conditions. This places the performer and the producer in a weak position. Waiting for the magic to happen by haphazard doodling or by the ritual of a repetitive warming up process, is a precarious business. What if nothing happens? In order therefore to be sure that something will happen, one must needs try to find a way for being able to call up in oneself what lies already there. What this thing is or where it comes from has been the subject of conjecture for every artist, philosopher and psychologist. What is more important is to establish the fact that nothing can be called out of oneself that is not already there.

In the welter of new methods, approaches, waves, experiments, that have filled the theatre of today, much has been claimed for the value of each as a means for " getting something out " of the actor. Any teacher or producer who can bring about a cathartic act of release in his students or actors, will be sure of a great following for a time. Many teachers appear to depend upon this very process themselves to " get something out " Whilst this process of mutual stimulation may produce something at each engagement, it does not of itself lay the foundation for calling up the magic in oneself, but only for the need for further sessions of mutual stimulation. The kind of stimulation that promotes the actor to get to work on himself, would seem to be of more practical use.

My experience in Cape Town was the culmination of my four years collaboration with Gerald Wragg and a confirmation of my belief that we must face up to this challenge of the creative life of the individual. Whether in the theatre, the class room, the studio or the workshop, we must concern ourselves with the person from within and the means he is employing to gain his ends. Aldous Huxley, Stanislavsky, Gordon Craig and Matthias Alexander have all been confronted with a great confusion between ends and means and each has made a great contribution in his own field. I think that we are getting nearer to a general understanding of the common need for us all, in whatever field we live and work. We must create or die.

CHAPTER VIII

MOVEMENT FOR ACTORS

I do not know what acting is, in the way that I know what dancing, singing and painting are. I only know that when I am present at the performance of a play, I am watching the conflict of two realities. There is the worldly reality of things that happen as they do, and the greater reality of the stage, which makes us feel why they happen, and how they happen, and shows us what goes on underneath the mask of real reality. I do not feel this conflict in dancing, or singing, or painting, because I am familiar with the symbols of ordered movement, sound and colour, and I can learn to understand and accept their intrinsic meaning.

I am confused when I see real people behaving like themselves in an obviously non-real setting. To what am I to open my mind and heart: to the painted tree or pillar, the reality of the bones and muscles of the players, the sound and meaning of the words, or to some other mystical thing that is born by the coming together of these component parts? And then one all too rare day, I see an actor disappear in what he is doing, and he lets me see through him to the other reality. I do not see Mr. X. giving a lovely performance of Hamlet, or Mr. Y. exhibiting his ability to make me laugh, but I have evoked in me some remembered experience of myself and other people, and I am made more alive in that moment. And I wonder again what acting is?

Since finishing the first edition of this book, I have come much more closely into contact with actors in a way that I had only experienced with dancers, and I have got to know their world from inside. The same softening of the edges of clearly defined styles and categories has taken place here as elsewhere, and influences from outside have left similar marks. Since the time when acting was a job to be learned by doing it, and when the actor-manager was the king pin around which a supporting company revolved, changes of organisation, style and conception, have been brought about by the initial ideas of one or two men.

The names of Stanislavsky, Edward Gordon Craig, and Rudolf Laban, will be familiar to all drama students, with perhaps a thought on the side for Delsarte. Three of these names have become associated with a system or a method. Edward Gordon Craig's influence has been through ideas, ideals, outrageous suggestion and impracticable projects. Yet each one of these men looked for the same thing and each took his own way in the search. Each wanted a better theatre, a truer theatre, a living theatre of the future through a greater understanding of his own time, and each man had a passion for, and a vision of, the theatre as an elemental power. Each man set his life to working towards this vision, and each found an answer in a study of man himself and his own personal activity as the generating force for the great art of the theatre.

Stanislavsky devised exercises for enabling the actor to produce the physical performance necessary to embody the character revealed by the text. Delsarte, a singing teacher, classified the connection between the physical areas of the body and the expressive implications of their design and mechanics. Laban reclassified movement in terms of mental and physical attitudes to environment, and analysed in elemental terms, the nature of movement and its cause and effect upon the spirit. Gordon Craig visualised an actor who could neutralise himself from realistic habit reactions and the impediment of personal emotions. His Uber-Marionette must be realised in the completely selfless and depersonalised actor, who can use himself as an empty vehicle for the passage of his imagination. It seems that Graig points to the heights, and guides Stanislavsky and Laban, the workers in the field, who have forged tools and implements for the climb, and who themselves saw to what purposes these tools could be put.

The work of Stanislavsky and Laban have had many more followers, imitators and disciples, than that of Craig or Delsarte, although the Delsarte system has been absorbed into many activities in America and at the beginning of the century many people were to be found " doing their Delsarte ". The present-day drama student " does his Stanislavsky " and " does his Movement . . . Laban type ", as a necessary part of his training as an actor.

Since the drama school, rather than the touring company or the repertory theatre, became the nursery for actors, Drama has assumed a subtle difference from Acting, in much the same way as Dance has different connotations from Dancing. One needs to be reminded that the act of doing is the final aim, and the ideas, thoughts, feelings, inspirations and visions about drama, dance and theatre, are concerned ultimately with an activity. Both Craig and Stanislavsky emphasised the need for the physical act of doing. Laban finalised his ideas about movement in the theatre, as a result of watching people in the act of doing.

Modern theatre is full of doing. Movement is everywhere, experiment and personal experience, individual truth and group stimulation abound. Plays no longer rely upon words that are delivered with size, panache and grandeur, befitting the god-like actor manager. The external form in the theatre has changed as rapidly as the skyline and the fashion trend, and the actor has to learn as many different styles or techniques to keep in touch with modern life. The drama student learns a little ballet, singing, fencing, national, historical and modern dance, mime, limbering, period movement, and in addition " does movement ". He learns how to behave in certain conventions and how to act in the Brechtian or Stanislavsky way. He studies classical acting and modern styles, and the list of required angles gets longer while the demands made upon his mental and physical mobility get heavier. He must say more, do more, in the attempt to find his own truth. He begins to learn to make use of the theatre for his own purposes; to turn it into a pulpit, a lecture platform, a political soap box or a national symbol. He finds that he can use it to exhibit himself and his problems in art whilst he seeks to find art in himself. And none of this was intended by the great reformers of the theatre.

The Method, in many hands, is a travesty of understanding of what Stanislavsky meant by the inner technique and the inner truth. Advocates of free movement have, in many cases, misused Laban's work in mistaking cause for effect. The work of Gordon Craig has been overlooked or passed by in general, as having nothing very much to do with modern theatre. And yet somewhere there is a connection between the work of these men and the strivings of modern drama and acting. Somewhere a co-ordinating factor is awaited.

I have spent a lot of time in the last ten years looking at actors, listening to actors, and conducting movement classes for actors. I have talked and listened to teachers and producers of actors, and I have collaborated in productions of plays. I have come to some conclusions which may emerge in the following paragraphs.

Whatever personal or private conception the actor or producer has of the role or the play, he is limited to the only two means of expression available to him; that of sound or movement. These are the tools of his trade and every care is given by him and his teachers to the training of these commodities. Since the actor is not setting out to be a singer, a dancer, an acrobat, he is not concerned with taking the two fundamental activities of speaking and moving to a high level of specialisation, although it is obvious to him that the better performance in either field will put him ahead of the less able actor. But when he finds himself having to play the part of someone highly skilled in some such specialisation, he is faced with a dilemma. Must he train in all the skills and styles he is likely to encounter, so that he can pull out of the hat the relevant piece of learning, or is there a general all-round condition of training and learning that will enable him to get by with a few trick lessons from a specialised professional? As I mentioned earlier, the usual training comes out on the side of an elementary introduction to a large number of skills, with a preponderance of training in movement and voice. In theory this seems to be logical, and since these two basic activities are fundamental to all other arts, it would seem infallible. Problems however do appear.

The actor is now very familiar with the methods and systems he has come to rely upon to get him nearer to the enrichment he seeks in his work. Actors are always open to new ideas, uninhibited in their response, aware of the need to equate acting with movement, and dedicated to the cause of self improvement. They are knowledgeable about Laban's analysis of movement and in many cases have adopted it with considerable effect to production and character. Their use of The Method, admittedly controversial, is very widespread in some form or another and their approach to text is greatly influenced by Stanislavsky's writings and the interpreters of his words. Improvisation and experiment have become the core of the actors' group work, and workshop productions are established as public tryouts. The New Theatre is now so recognisable in format as to be in danger of being old hat. Meanwhile the many classical revivals and the eternal challenge and delight of Shakespeare, makes ever-increasing demands upon the actor for a range of understanding and ability matched only by the span of Drama itself. And in the midst of this torrent of dramatic activity and possibility stands the person of the actor with the sole instrument of himself.

This person in the actor gives him a lot of trouble. He must be concerned with the person of the character even while he is trying to keep connected to himself. A lot has been said and written about the personality of the actor and the place of emotions in the business of acting. I have found young actors appalled to discover that acting, like any other activity, is a job to be done. They are confused by injuctions not to emote, to get on with the job, and a little later to be told to infuse some feeling into their technical exercises. It is difficult to help an actor towards a rounded sense of himself as a think-feel instrument when the very word feel has so many connotations.

In using movement as part of an actor's training, one is setting out to do two things. The actor needs to have a vocabulary of movements and gestures which have been systemised, for effective use and reference. The analysis of Rudolf Laban gives a very rich index of movement patterns, habits and expressive indications, and offers to the producer, choreographer and actor, a vast amount of material for dramatic use. It reveals the whole nature of movement and its manifestation in human expression, but the actor still needs to be in a condition to be able to produce at will the movement patterns and thought feelings intrinsic to the character he is playing. In addition to gaining a vocabulary and an insight through movement, the actor has to be able to relinquish any habit pattern of his own that would be unsuitable for the character being played. And here comes the pinch. How can he be sure not only of removing unwanted patterns of habit, but patterns of thinking and feeling, when the whole structure of his working life has been built upon such patterning. The greatest value of movement training for the actor, in my opinion, is that, sooner or later, it does reveal the constant and unchanging manner in which the actor handles himself in the course of his daily activity. Unfortunately this very fact has been used considerably to classify individuals in terms of types, and to hasten highly coloured conclusions in terms of ability, promise and personality, with very disappointing results when these potentials seem to come to a stop. What is more important is to try to teach the actor how he can improve his general use of himself in everyday activities.

I have found that "good movers" are very often very inadequate non-movers. That an enormously rich vocabulary of things to do does not of itself help the actor to be still with conviction and confidence. That feeling emotionally and feeling physically are very often confused by the actor, and that he does not know whether what he is feeling emotionally is coming through suitably in physical terms. And I have found that a great deal of the actor's problems can be summed up as follows.

In playing a character, the actor must be able to see that character in his mind's eye and be able to work him out into physical reality and action. All the actor's training will be there to help him to call upon material, but in the event, he has to be able to connect up within himself the physical feel of his imagination. At this stage, his own emotions are an impediment. The idea of the character and the physical feel of the character in terms of the body, must be welded together before the emotions can be generated. What the actor has to be sure of is the reliabilty of his own physical or muscular feelings. This is the problem that comes to light in nine cases out of ten.

The actor discovers that he cannot feel his own complete muscular condition, either at rest or in action, until he has managed to get beyond or behind the subconscious handling of himself without thought or true feeling. The great performers in all time, have been able to call up intuitively or instinctively the image of the character, and have only then to work upon this in their own way. In most cases however, the actor relies upon a technique or procedure that has been taught to him or that he has found works for him. In my own experience as a person, a teacher, a producer and a performer, I have found it necessary to look for a technique within myself to enable me to make use of whatever material lies to hand.

The result of finding a personal technique reduces unnecessary activity to a minimum and releases whatever mental and physical energy there is available, towards the required goal. This in some measure comes to the aid of the actor in his dilemma of how much to specialise in how many things he may be called upon to do or know, and how to find time for everything. It also brings movement training into direct line with thinking, so that with the practice of a personal technique, the actor is improving his ability to lend himself to specialised techniques of speaking and moving that will be unencumbered by the luggage of habit.

What this personal technique is and how it can be employed is the special interest and activity of Gerald Wragg, to whom I referred in the previous chapter. Mr. Wragg has kindly contributed a final chapter to the new edition, but I want to finish the present chapter with a complete quotation of a very early essay of his which sums up for me my own experiences and thoughts about acting and the theatre. In my long teaching life with dancers, singers, actors, painters and people, and in my meeting with the great names of the theatre, either in the flesh or through their writings, I have found the constant for which the search goes on, to be vested within each person and in man's ability to elevate himself through art to the conception of divine perfection.

WITCHCRAFT IN THE THEATRE
By Gerald Wragg

An essay on experiment in Theatre

Are we searching for a New Theatre, or are we seeking that which will enable us to give due expression to our great dramatic heritage and that which will cause us to show to our fellows that we are at one in spirit with Shakespeare, with Racine, with the Greeks?

L'art nouveau is a myth. Worse, it is a snare and a delusion.

There is nothing new under the sun. Why then do we seek it?
Because our theatre has creaked its way to a stop; because our
society has become static; and we are provoked by its banality to
a frenzied search for something new to prove that life, that the
theatre, is important, means something, has content.

Are we mad? Or do we possess the ineffable wisdom of the
mystic, the knowingness of the witch? We know that we are mad
to know, to be wise. So we put on masks and practise the magic
rites of improvisation; we place ourselves as sacrificial crumbs
upon the alter of Golden Mean-ness, and hope that we shall
happen to become generous through our trans-substantiation.

This is not making theatre. It is merely making ourselves
theatrical. We cannot justify these weird practices on the grounds
that we are being creative, for the art of the actor is not
creative. Creativity in the theatre is solely the field of the
dramatist, the musician, the choreographer. The director,
designer, actor are there to interpret the art in theatrical terms.

Let us delude ourselves no further. The crux of the matter is
that we have lost the skill of acting. Our ambition may be great,
we may believe that we have a valuable contribution to make in
the theatre, but we don't know how to do it. Whether we
realise it or not, we are experimenting to recover something that
has been lost.

We cannot evolve new forms of theatrical expression; we
can only develop those which exist, which have always existed.
And we cannot develop them if we cannot command them. By
and large, we have lost command of the actor's most expressive
instrument—voice. " Breathless we stand when feeling most " ...
Byron. We have lost dignity of posture, grace and flexibility of
movement. We mumble and scream, we slouch and rigidise, we
shuffle and jerk, we act naturally, God help us, and we elevate
nothing. We are killing the theatre by being unable to give life to
our great dramas, and by working through our miserable
mumblings and slouchings, the degrading and demoralising
gibberish of the no-dramatist. We have forgotten that man is a
unique being and that man made the theatre. What then have we
lost? We have lost our uniqueness, our essential unity of function
and behaviour. The theatre is the quintessence of human life,

the expression of man's essential uniqueness. We must recover our uniqueness, our essential unity of function and behaviour if we are once again to breath life into our art. We have the imagination, the appreciation of our great dramatic heritage; we must become once again integrated ourselves, so that we may become at one, not in spirit merely, but in action, with Shakespeare, with Racine, with the Greeks. We must elevate ourselves to that level of understanding which is thought in action. We must integrate in order to co-ordinate.

For co-ordinate is what we must do. We must co-ordinate ourselves in order to recover command. Command of voice, posture, movement, the material of the actor's interpretive art. For make no mistake, the interpretive art is wider, more comprehensive than the art of the creator of art. We must learn to command our use of ourselves in such a way that our function is most efficient, and since we are a unique organism, we must co-ordinate in use in order to function as a unit.

We can use our masks when, and only when, the mask transforms the whole actor. We can improvise when, and only when, the whole person can react as a whole, to the stimulus of the unknown. We can use the law of the Golden Mean as a natural law when, and only when we function truly naturally; when we use ourselves according to the law of our own nature, which is that of a unique being.

We must learn the way to co-ordinate ourselves, and there is a way which may be learned and there are teachers to teach it—but it is a hard way; it is in itself an act of creation and true creation is an act of faith. Belief is a thought; Faith is an Act.

CHAPTER IX

A TECHNIQUE FOR PERFORMANCE
By Gerald Wragg

We hear a good deal these days from actors and performers generally of the need to relax, to release the imagination, to become involved, and so on. To these purposes " situations " are contrived, exercises devised, " happenings " arranged, to such an extent that style of performance in general is influenced and even radically changed by the experiences undergone, and the original purpose is lost or forgotten. To my mind this is a confusion of ends and means.

Presumably, when a performer decides he needs to relax, it is because he is dissatisfied with the *results* of what he is doing. His conception of the character and style of his task, whether it be a " part " in a play or opera, a song or a piece of instrumental music, may be quite satisfactory, but something prevents him from realising his conception; something gets in the way. This something, he may conclude, is " tension "; he must learn to relax. Or he may find in the course of his unsuccessful attempts that his conception has become blurred or lost altogether, and he decides that his imagination is inhibited; he must learn to release it. Or again, he may fail to see that something is getting in the way, but rather decide that he is *positively* failing to identify himself with his purpose; he must *do something*; he must become " involved ".

Given a necessary minimum of talent, which he presumably possesses or he would not have decided to become a performer, and without which no kind or amount of training will be of any avail, it is far more likely that his problem is one of interference rather than positive failure to do whatever is required, and this interference, which he may call tension, anxiety, faulty co-ordination, inhibition, can always be shown to have as a basis a *general muscular over-activity*. Where this pertains, the person may be said to be more or less in a state of stress.

The concept of mind-body unity, the total interdependence o f mind and muscle, is now a widely accepted tenet of education and training, although the practical implications are by no means sufficiently understood. Electromyographic techniques have made clear beyond dispute that " Tout état intillectuel est accompagné de manifestations physiques determinées "; furthermore, that it is impossible to conceive an activity without causing minute responses in those muscles which carry out the activity in reality. It would seem, then, that in any problem of performance, the muscular aspect must be taken into account, and given at least as close a study as is nowadays generally given to the psychological factors involved.

In my experience the study of physiology is of no value in dealing with the *practical* problems of stress, since it is entirely theoretical, and suggests no *technique* for discovering in what muscle groups reflex responses are occurring at any given moment, (but only in which they could occur), nor for measuring the degree of tension for the purpose of deciding whether it is excessive or not. Only in the examination of the living individual in action can this be done. Nor does the study of physiology suggest any means for *re-education* in those cases where muscular over-activity (stress) habitually characterises the manner of use of the individual.

The practice of movement or relaxation exercises begs the question, for these are performances in themselves, and as such are simply reproductions of the same muscular response patterns, and in those cases where problems of performance exist, *the same stress situations*, that the exercises are designed to improve or correct.

Muscular over-activity (stress) can be of two kinds: (i) a local over-activity in specific mechanisms, (ii) a general over-activity throughout the system. The first is easily understood in terms such as writer's cramp, pianist's wrist, tennis elbow, etc., though by the time these symptons reveal themselves the tension is particularly excessive. The second is more difficult to define, for it is a condition of which the individual is more or less unaware (in fact the greater the over-tension the less aware he is), whilst his teachers and doctors, though they may be aware of it, are not by their training adequately equipped to make an accurate diagnosis of general over-activity, or to provide a remedy. The basis for an accurate diagnosis lies in a knowledge of what F. Matthias Alexander called the Primary Control, that is the relationship of the head to the neck and these to the back, and which acts as a kind of master-reflex for the whole body. Where the Primary Control is mis-used, the individual operates in a more or less un-co-ordinated manner; the spine tends to be unduly curved, the thorax lacks mobility, the joints are restricted due to over-contraction pulling the joint surfaces towards each other. Balance is impaired, and vocal function is reduced. Any individual who habitually mis-uses the Primary Control is therefore constantly functioning on a lower level than that of which he is capable. The influence of this relatively uncontrolled manner of use is all the time working on the system as a whole, making modifications which show themselves first as physiological and emotional changes, and later as behavioural and structural changes.

Writer's cramp, tennis elbow, etc., already mentioned, are examples of physiological changes. Emotional changes are more subtle but no less real, since muscle is the means whereby emotional responses are made, not only in respect of emotional *attitudes* such as fear, aggression, timidity, but also in emotional *moods* such as depression, excitement, and so on. It is particularly necessary for actors, dancers, musicians, to understand this fact, for in each case the object of performance is the visual and aural expression of emotion. If the performer is in a state of over-tension *prior* to the expression of an emotion his expression will be restricted, " under-played ". If, as is more usual, he makes an effort to overcome his tension, the expression will be exaggerated. This condition of over-tension immediately prior to the performance of an act is more suitably called *pre-tension*; there is no room in art for pretence.

Of equal importance to the performer, and coming under the heading of " emotional changes ", is the part muscle plays in influencing the whole pattern of body behaviour through the kinaesthetic sense. Where the Primary Control is mis-used, the general level of tension throughout the system is more or less excessive, and the muscle to brain feed-back is impaired. In such a case the individual has little or no awareness of his body, so that any attempt he might make consciously to determine a kind or manner of body expression can only be a hit-and-miss business. This is a very common state of affairs among performers in all spheres, and most producers and teachers have experienced the situation in which a performer is told that he is making unwanted bodily movements, or stiffening some part of himself, and he denies this. Or, on being instructed to perform a certain movement, such as lifting his arm or bending his knees, he makes other movements at the same time which weaken the expression of the intended movement.

Behavioural changes are very common among performers, being what is often called " putting on an act ". For instance, a person who habitually squares his shoulders (at the expense of shortening his neck) will not be aware of the muscular act but is likely suddenly to become aware of a feeling of manliness, and from that moment on will consciously induce this feeling, i.e. will exaggerate the habitual use of himself, particularly when wishing to impress other people. Similarly, the following of fashion in behaviour, e.g. the so-called " camp " manner, has its origin in mis-use of the Primary Control, in that postural awareness is diminished to a point of depersonalisation, and the individual can assert himself only through the copying of another's behaviour.

" Structurally, muscle is not only capable of being modified itself, but also modifies the bones and joints on which it works, and the circulatory system which traverses it ", (Barlow). Habitual mis-use of the Primary Control exerts a constant detrimental influence on the structure of the individual, so that sooner or later his total shape is characterised by some deformity, e.g. protruding abdomen, hollow back, unduly curved upper spine. " Man is not bent because he is old but because his unconscious defences bend him ". An individual who has become structurally deformed, in however little or greater degree, is incapable of changing his total shape, that is his shape when in a condition of stillness, without straining; if he does change his shape, e.g. pull in his abdomen or try to straighten his spine, he will look unnatural, will be unable to maintain it for any length of time, and will move from this shape in a stiff and exaggerated manner. Incidentally, the performance of repetitive exercises has much the same effect of modifying the structure, hence the easily recognisable shape of the classical ballet dancer, and the consequent limitation of his or her movement expression. It is a point for consideration that the art for which such training was evolved has in turn become so influenced by the training that it has become unnatural.

In the foregoing paragraphs I have referred to the " habitual manner of use " of the individual. Let us now consider this term in detail. A human being does not passively react on a basis of stimulus-response as does an inanimate object such as, say, a coiled spring. This, being stretched or compressed, will, by its nature return to its normal condition, which we may call stasis, on being released. A human being is rather a *thinking* organism, concerned with the " organisation of preferred perception ". This may apply to any or all of three factors at any given moment: (i) the perception of a preferred body pattern (for example the crossing of one leg over another when sitting in a " relaxed " manner), (ii) preferred set of external circumstances, (iii) preferred inter-personal response. In this organisation of preferred perception, muscular activity plays its part, and the muscular responses by which a person adjusts to his environment invariably follows a built-in subconscious pattern, determined by heredity and enviromental influence; this invariable pattern is the habitual manner of use. For instance, when a person decides to sit down, the muscular activity by which the movement is carried out is not under his conscious direction, but automatically follows his own invariable habit pattern. He has no choice in the matter, is not likely to be aware of his muscular responses; he takes the act of sitting for granted, just as he does all his movement activities throughout the daily round. Furthermore the act of sitting will culminate in a state of non-movement (statis or posture), for however long or short a time elapses before another movement is made. The posture comes about as a result of the movement, so that if, for instance, the person has according to his habitual manner of use contracted his neck muscles and bent his spine, the resultant posture will be charact-erised by the shortened neck and curved spine, and the movement which comes out of this posture will, in its *manner* of being carried out, be determined by these characteristics of posture. We may make, then, the following proposition: all movement starts and ends in a posture, or resting state; this resting state and the movement which follows from it will be balanced or unbalanced according to the distribution of tension.

An unbalanced resting state is characterised by muscular over-tension this being the *residual* tension left over from the activity which preceded the resting state. Unless this over-tension is resolved (by returning to a balanced resting state), any activity which follows must inevitably be performed with excessive tension, i.e. it will be a stress activity, which, on completion will in its turn leave residual tension, and so the vicious cycle will continue. Where a person more or less fails to give a satisfactory performance, as fail he must if under stress, orthodox teaching attempts to solve the problem by positive instructions, *giving the person more to do than the performance originally entailed*, and thus increasing the stress. Most students will have experience of being less successful in some activity after training than they were before. Nor does the answer lie in abandoning the formal demands of the situation and allowing what is commonly called " free expression ". If residual tension is present, this will still be a stress activity, even though the absence of formal demands makes for an apparently freer performance; it is only a question of degree. Between rigidity and laissez-faire lies the broad middle course of re-education in the *commanding of the balanced resting state;* in other words the restoration of the Primary Control, and the gradual awakening of consciousness to its existence. This is not an easy rask, for it requires expert tuition from one who is in possession of his own primary control, conscious of it and practised in allowing it to work for him, and at the same time knowing the means whereby he can restore it in the pupil and teach him consciously to prevent interference with it. Furthermore, when a person is in a state of unresolved tension more or less constantly, there is a fear of returning to a balanced resting state, since this will involve the realisation of " true " emotional experience, and an adjusting of his picture of reality. The preferred image one has of oneself is usually maintained by organising one's muscular adjustment in a given way; by maintaining a state of unresolved tension it is possible to avoid being aware of the difference between the artificial picture one has of oneself, and the real picture which would emerge in the balanced resting state.

It is possible to teach a balanced resting state, so that from this point of vantage the pupil may realise what are the reactions which interfere with it; it is possible to impart a technique which gives the person the consciousness of a controlling factor hitherto unsuspected and which allows him a freedom and strength fully expressive of his intentions. As a result it is possible for him to develop such an awareness of himself in relation to his immediate environment that he knows exactly what to do at any given moment. In my belief it is this " presence of mind " coupled with freedom and command of action that, given the talent, characterises the performance of the outstanding artistes of any generation. It is said that great art can only come from a great age; I believe that great performance can come from any age if the manner of use of the means whereby of performance is suitably commanded.

Suggestions for further reading

Alexander F. M. *The Use of the Self*

Bowden George C., *F. Matthias Alexander and The Creative Advance of the Individual*